Liebe Frau Pomposo!

Mit diesem Andenken Deiner Heimatstadt, will ich vielen Dank sagen – für das geduldige Helfen meiner unzähligen Fragen zu beantworten und für das Tutoring von letztem Semester. Ich habe so viel von Dir gelernt.

Mit herzlichen Grüssen,

David

MUNICH

By George Bailey
and the Editors of Time-Life Books

With photographs by Stefan Moses

THE GREAT CITIES · TIME-LIFE BOOKS · AMSTERDAM

The Author: George Bailey is a graduate of Columbia College, New York City, and Magdalen College, Oxford. He has spent 35 years in Europe, most of them in Germany and Austria. During the Second World War he served as an American Army intelligence and liaison officer and was interpreter-translator for the U.S.S.R. and Germany at the surrender negotiations. In 1959 he won the Overseas Press Club Award for magazine reporting on foreign affairs. He is the author of the best-selling book *Germans.*

The Photographer: Stefan Moses was born in Germany in 1928. In 1948 he became a stage photographer with the Weimar National Theatre. He moved to Munich in 1950, and has since gained international experience working as a magazine photographer. His work has been shown at many exhibitions, and five books of his photographs have been published, including the recent *Deutsche.*

TIME-LIFE BOOKS
EUROPEAN EDITOR: Kit van Tulleken
Design Director: Louis Klein
Photography Director: Pamela Marke
Chief of Research: Vanessa Kramer
Special Projects Editor: Windsor Chorlton
Chief Sub-Editor: Ilse Gray

THE GREAT CITIES
Series Editor: Deborah Thompson
Editorial Staff for *Munich*
Text Editor: Jane Havell
Designer: Joyce Mason
Picture Editor: Caroline Alcock
Staff Writer: Louise Earwaker
Text Researchers: Toni Huberman, Elizabeth Loving
Senior Sub-Editor: Nicoletta Flessati
Design Assistants: Paul Reeves, Adrian Saunders
Editorial Assistant: Kathryn Coutu
Proof-Reader: Aquila Kegan

Editorial Production:
Chief: Ellen Brush
Traffic Co-ordinator: Linda Mallett
Picture Department: Sarah Dawson
Art Department: Julia West
Editorial Department: Debra Lelliott, Ajaib Singh Gill

The captions and the texts accompanying the photographs in this volume were prepared by the editors of Time-Life Books.

Published by Time-Life Books (Nederland) B.V.
Ottho Heldringstraat 5, Amsterdam 1018.

ISBN 7054 0503 6

Cover: A medley of architectural forms and colours in the centre of Munich's old city is dominated (left) by the orange-tiled tower of the Altes Rathaus (Old Town Hall), a 15th-Century building remodelled in 1968. The copper-domed tower of a city-centre bank (right), built in 1907, contrasts with an office block (background) in modern style.

First end paper: A typical sight in Munich's beer-halls and gardens, 10 foaming litres stand ready for consumption. This brew, known as Märzenbier and traditionally brewed in the month of March, is one of the many seasonal beers for which Munich breweries are world-famous.

Last end paper: Two dancers, their classical robes swirling, grace a wall in the villa that belonged to one of Munich's greatest artists, Franz von Stuck. A major German exponent of Symbolist art, Stuck created this gold-painted plaster panel in 1896 as part of the decorations for his home, now a museum of his work.

Contents

I

The Best of Bavaria

I approached Munich for the first time from the best of all possible viewpoints—the north. The panorama before me on that spring day was spectacular. The city rose from a foreground of gently rolling, plush green meadows that were patched by forests—well-spaced battalions of pine, beech, spruce and larch, with occasional sturdy oaks and slender birches. Behind the city, stretching the length of the horizon, stood in serried ranks the Alps—abrupt, arresting and majestic in their greatcoats of snow.

Military metaphors came naturally to me then, for the year was 1945 and I had come to Munich as a lieutenant in the U.S. Army, acting as a liaison officer among the various forces since I was fluent in both Russian and German. I arrived to find what had been one of the most beautiful cities in the world reduced to empty, shattered buildings and nine million cubic yards of rubble that still filled the air with dust. One-sixth of the city's buildings had been totally destroyed and many more damaged beyond redemption. The serene squares and airy esplanades that had made Munich so graceful were little more than junkyards. In the oldest part of the city the 15th-Century Frauenkirche—the cathedral that was Munich's traditional symbol—had been gutted by fire-bombs. For the moment, Munich seemed a corpse. It was impossible for me to see beneath the shroud of dust and debris to a city that was, at heart, still its living self.

But, looking back, even worse than the physical destruction that impeded my appreciation of Munich was the bitter resentment left in me by the war: for an inescapable part of the ideological debris of the Third Reich was the fact that Munich was too much Adolf Hitler's town. Here the National Socialist Party had been founded, here Hitler engineered his first attempt to grasp political power. From here and the surrounding regions Hitler drew many of his notorious lieutenants. At Dachau, close outside the city, was an infamous concentration camp. And the very name of Munich had become the symbol, after the Hitler-Chamberlain agreement of 1938, for the legalized rape of Czechoslovakia.

Everything I saw seemed to combine to emphasize only the most recent past. It happened, for example, that one of the historic buildings in central Munich to remain comparatively unscathed was the Feldherrnhalle (Hall of Heroes), a pillared memorial copied from the 14th-Century Loggia dei Lanzi in Florence. It was built in the 1840s to honour two generals, and a memorial to the Bavarian Army was added in 1892. But its symbolism had been converted in the public imagination to the cause of the Nazis. In 1923 the blood of some of Hitler's fellow putschists had been shed in front of its

Dressed in traditional finery for the Oktoberfest, the city's world-famous annual beer festival, this cheery cigar-puffing driver of a Munich beer cart shows all the robust good humour of the Bavarian countryman. Behind him can just be glimpsed the beer barrels gaily garlanded with white flowers by the brewery for the occasion.

steps when the police fired on the Nazis' marching column in order to shatter their first mass demonstration of strength.

In the weeks and months that followed my arrival I slowly began to see through the pall of physical destruction and the distortion of my own prejudices, and to revise my opinion of the city. True, there was some foundation of knowledge on which I could build. As a child, I had spent enchanting holidays in the wild, primeval forests of Washington State in north-west America. The game-warden I used to stay with was a German; from him and his friends I learnt the language at an early age.

From that idyllic time onwards, finding out about the country and the culture that had nurtured those solitary, self-sufficient forest-dwellers had been a passion with me. And I was already aware that Munich enjoyed a unique reputation as a city of the arts and of artists. It had been frequented by Mozart, cultivated by Wagner, beloved by Thomas Mann.

Indeed, a few such links with the past still remained. One of my first memories of Munich is of the octogenarian composer Richard Strauss, who would stroll through the rubble, picking his way with his cane, to greet American soldiers with the statement in English: "I am the author of *Der Rosenkavalier*." He was fêted by everyone who loved his great romantic opera; I was struck by the totality of his exemption from the Americans' general censure of Germans.

But all this was superficial—mere background, first impressions. I lacked the essential element for deeper understanding: extended experience of the people and of the city in peacetime.

The first Münchner I really got to know was introduced to me by a mutual friend in the first winter after the war. One of my colleagues was William Sloane Coffin, Jr., later to become chaplain of Yale University and famous in America as an outspoken opponent of the Vietnam War. Then a young lieutenant, he went on leave to a Bavarian Alpine village for the express purpose of learning to ski. His ski instructor was Sepp Kessler, a former sergeant in the *Gebirgsjäger*—a crack ski-troop of the German Army. Sepp was a superb athlete, a walking monument to Bavarian manhood in all typical respects save one: he was, unusually, a teetotaller. Sepp taught Coffin to ski and also gave him a lesson in clean, strenuous living. Coffin returned to our headquarters singing the praises of Alpine life in general and of Sepp in particular. The next summer we happened to meet Sepp in Munich: as usual in summer—always a bad season for skiers and instructors—he was filling in time.

"What are you doing for a living?" asked Coffin.

"I'm a bartender at an American officers' club," said Sepp.

"You're a what?" queried Coffin in astonishment. "But you don't know anything about mixing drinks; you never took a drink in your life!"

"That's right," said Sepp, "But it didn't take long to learn. I'll never forget my first customer. He was an American major. He came up to the bar and

A giant pretzel proves more than a mouthful for this young visitor to the Auer Dult, a market fair held three times a year in south-east Munich. Pretzels—savoury bread twists sprinkled with cumin seeds—are part of the Münchner's staple diet. A traditional accompaniment to beer, they are on sale in all sizes at major festivities.

said, 'Gimme a horse's neck.' I said, 'A horse's neck coming up, sir,' and turned around to the array of bottles on the shelves behind me. I grabbed two or three of them at random, poured something from each one into a shaker with some ice in it, poured the mixture into a glass and handed it to the major. He took a gulp and spewed it out all over the bar. 'What the hell is this?' he roared. 'That, sir,' I said, 'is a Bavarian horse's neck.' 'A *Bavarian* horse's neck?' said the major incredulously, 'Here, let me show you how to make a real American horse's neck!' He did, and so I had my first recipe. My second customer was a captain who wanted a dry martini. Of course, he got a Bavarian dry martini. And so it went. It was easy."

Such was one of numerous encounters that introduced me to the nature of the Bavarians: their resilience, their resourcefulness, their unshakable, unapologetic sense of identity. *"Mir san Mir!"* (We are we!), as they say in Bavarian dialect, in their gentle, relaxed accent which has more in common with that of their Alpine neighbours, the Austrians, than with the clipped and rapidly spoken German that is heard in the north.

Munich itself began to regain its qualities one by one, so that my knowledge of the city and its own physical and psychological recovery advanced side by side. But economic recovery took rather longer. One of the worst shortages, lasting more than three years, was food. As a result, when the U.S. Army commandeered countless houses and many thousands of the best apartments in Munich, such appropriation was not always unwelcome. Often it meant that the owners or occupants on whom the troops were imposed were assured of sharing army rations, which were vastly superior in quality to anything available in Germany. My unit of eight men lived in a three-storey, three-family house and we fed ourselves as well as at least 20 Germans on our more than ample normal rations.

The American Army took command of all rubble-removal operations, supplying trucks, gasoline, coal and even manpower. Track was laid to transport the rubble for dumping to the north of the city. But there was a limit to what the Americans could do on their own, and the Münchners had been brought, by war and starvation, to such a weakened and listless state that average individual work capacity was reduced to about one-third of normal. In the three years following the war, only 700 new apartments were built in the city. As elsewhere in Germany—still at that time under the separate administrations of American, British, French and Soviet military agencies—there was virtually no productive capacity to underpin the economy and no faith in the currency; cigarettes were stronger units of exchange than Deutschmarks.

All this improved in 1948. In that year the three Western administrations agreed to merge their zones, in effect creating present-day West Germany. On June 18, they introduced a new currency. Already, America's European Recovery Program, devised by U.S. Secretary of State George Marshall, was pumping billions of dollars into the country. Almost overnight,

Patterns of Past and Present

Munich's development over a span of eight centuries is clearly reflected in the layout of its streets today. Surrounding the city centre is the Altstadtring (Old Town Ring), the inner ring road (brown in main map and inset) built along the line of the walls that contained Munich in the 14th Century. Within this ring stand such buildings as the extensive Residenz palace and the Frauenkirche, Munich's twin-towered cathedral.

Only in the 1800s, when the Electorate of Bavaria became a kingdom, did the city burst its ancient confines. New suburbs, containing the imposing Ludwigstrasse and the Königsplatz, were created to the north and west. In addition, the construction of a bridge, the Ludwigsbrücke, allowed the city's expansion eastwards over the River Isar. Linking these areas to the centre are roads that radiate outwards to the Mittlerer Ring (Middle Ring road), shown inset (tan). On the far side of this thoroughfare have sprung up the city's post-Second World War industrial and residential suburbs.

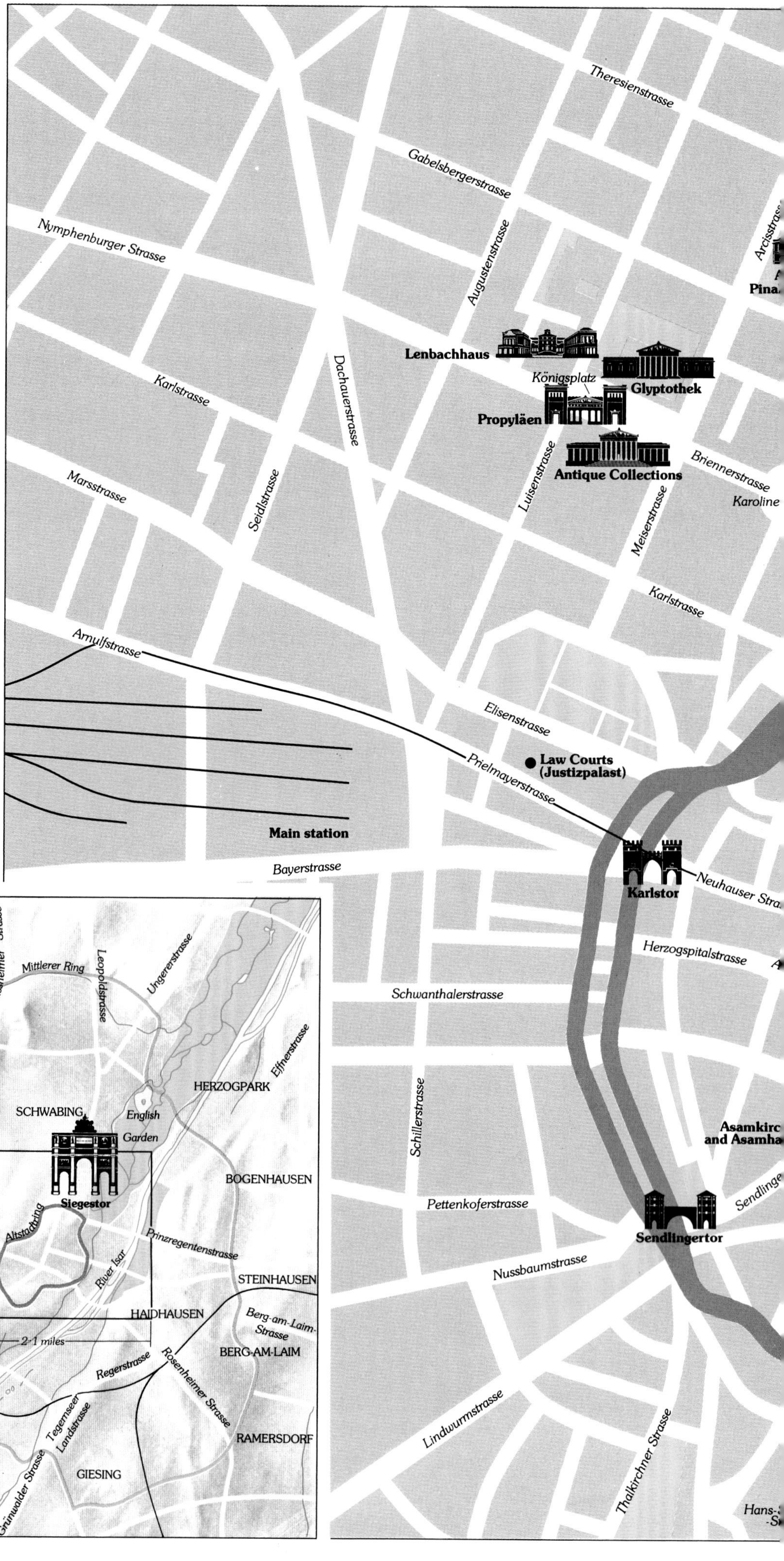

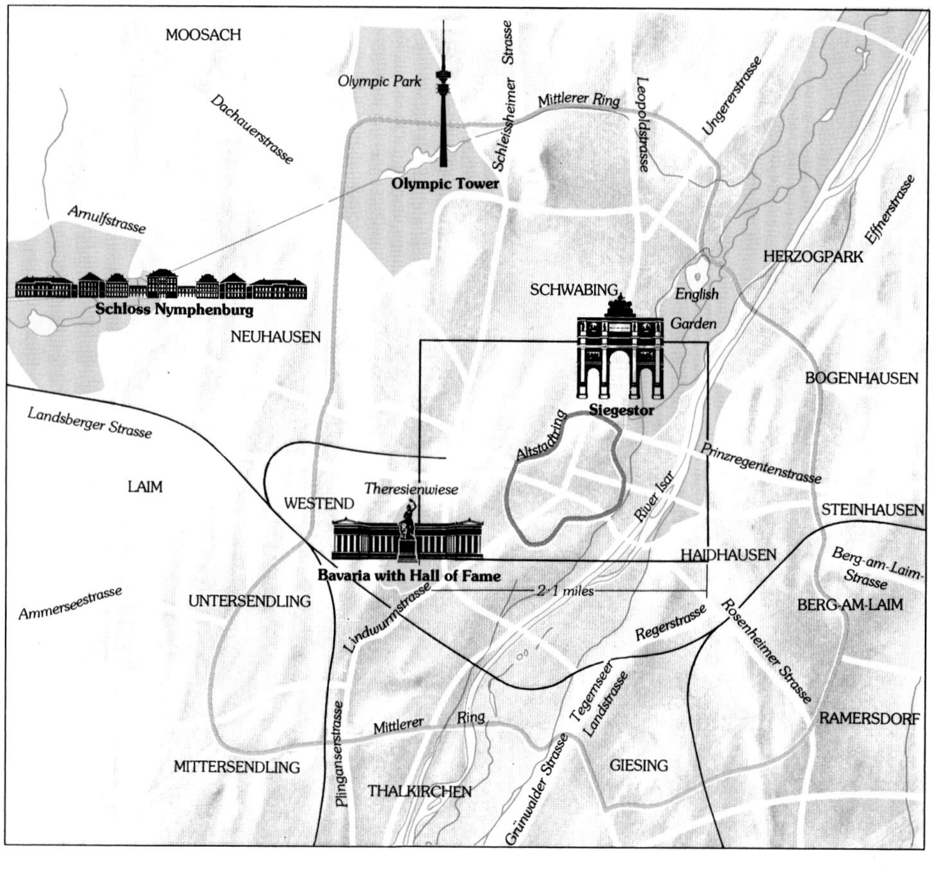

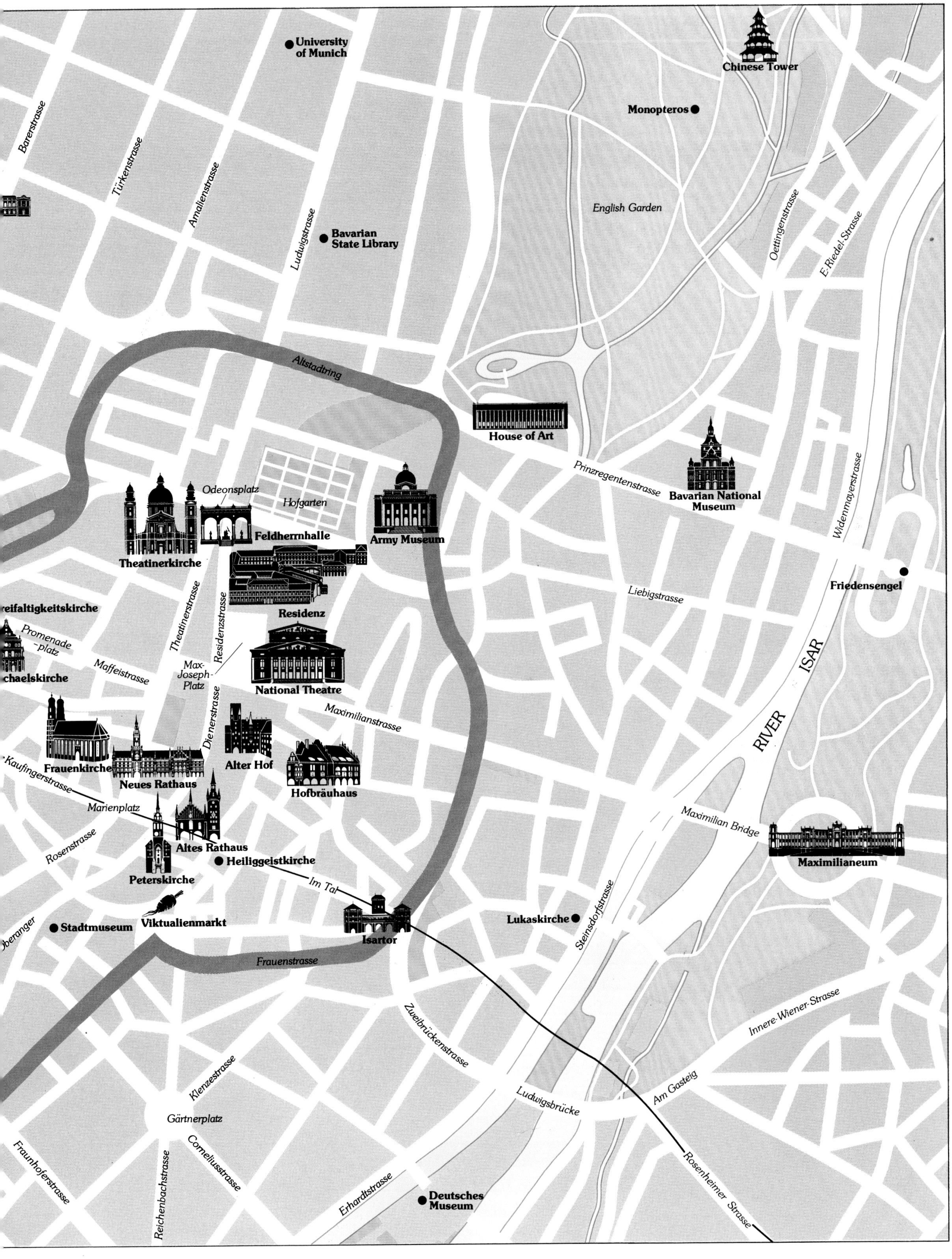
University of Munich
Chinese Tower
Monopteros
Barerstrasse
Türkenstrasse
Amalienstrasse
Ludwigstrasse
Bavarian State Library
English Garden
Oettingenstrasse
E.-Riedel-Strasse
Altstadtring
House of Art
Bavarian National Museum
Prinzregentenstrasse
Widenmayerstrasse
Odeonsplatz
Hofgarten
Theatinerkirche
Feldherrnhalle
Army Museum
Friedensengel
Liebigstrasse
Residenz
reifaltigkeitskirche
Promenade-platz
Theatinerstrasse
Residenzstrasse
Maffeistrasse
Max-Joseph-Platz
National Theatre
chaelskirche
RIVER ISAR
Maximilianstrasse
Dienerstrasse
Alter Hof
Frauenkirche
Neues Rathaus
Hofbräuhaus
Kaufingerstrasse
Marienplatz
Maximilian Bridge
Maximilianeum
Rosenstrasse
Altes Rathaus
Heiliggeistkirche
Peterskirche
Im Tal
Lukaskirche
Steinsdorfstrasse
Oberanger
Stadtmuseum
Viktualienmarkt
Isartor
Frauenstrasse
Innere-Wiener-Strasse
Zweibrückenstrasse
Klenzestrasse
Ludwigsbrücke
Am Gasteig
Gärtnerplatz
Fraunhoferstrasse
Corneliusstrasse
Reichenbachstrasse
Erhardtstrasse
Deutsches Museum
Rosenheimer Strasse

confidence revived, despite the fact that the Soviets at once clamped down on their own zone—present-day East Germany. The principal author of the currency reform—the rotund, prosperous-looking Ludwig Erhard—became Finance Minister and piloted Germany into its "economic miracle" of the 1950s, of which Munich was very much a part.

As if by magic, in the markets and shops of Germany there suddenly appeared a shimmering abundance of wares and produce. A major sensation for the Germans—who, like the British, were starved of sweets—was the spectacular reappearance of the great variety of pastries for which Germany is renowned; and nowhere did they seem so sumptuous and so excellent as in Munich. As far as I was concerned, Munich became overnight the world capital of pastry. I was entranced by the fresh warm smell of baking that every morning pervaded the Marienplatz, the city's central square. The experience affected other walks of life. From then on, I saw the baroque style of Bavarian architecture—rich with voluptuous white-and-gold cloud-forms interspersed with golden sunburst patterns—as vast quantities of cream shot through with lightning flashes of caramel.

I also rapidly discovered, as things got back to normal, that all Munich's food rivalled Vienna's for the prize of the best inland cuisine in Europe. The Münchners are anything but vegetarian. "The best vegetable is meat," they say dismissively, and their preferred meats are pork and veal. *Schweinernes*—any part of the pig—is a favourite with Bavarians, whether the pork is fresh, pickled or smoked. A popular dish is *Gselchtes*, mildly smoked pork, often eaten as a snack with coarse peasant bread and washed down with a litre of beer. The veal recipe that I like best is *Kalbshaxe*, a knuckle of veal simmered with pickled cucumber. But you can also have *Kalbshaxe* braised, roasted, stuffed, or breadcrumbed and fried. Then there are the sausages, especially Munich's own *Weisswürste*, which are made from a combination of finely ground fresh veal and pork. Custom dictates that *Weisswürste* must be served with a special light sweet mustard and eaten by noon on the day they are made. Another popular snack is *Leberkäs*, which translates as "liver cheese", although it is not made of cheese and need not be made of liver. It is actually a spiced minced meat loaf—usually beef, pork or bacon. Served piping hot, with mustard, bread and beer, it is a meal in itself, but is usually treated as a mere *Schmankerl*—a titbit.

The problem of reconstituting Munich after the war was, of course, a far more serious business than arranging the reappearance of goods in the shops. The city had to rebuild itself. Laudably, it set about the task of restoring damaged buildings wherever possible, instead of sweeping them away and replacing them with modern structures—a policy established in principle by the Lord Mayor of Munich, Dr. Karl Scharnagl, in 1947. "Munich," he said, "will hold fast to its traditional cosiness." Scharnagl spoke for the majority of Münchners. In 1949 the city announced a contest for the best

After heavy air raids during the Second World War, the domed towers of Munich's cathedral, the Frauenkirche, rise above the ruins of nearby bombed buildings. A Munich landmark since the 15th Century, the Frauenkirche towers survived the war though the cathedral itself was hit by fire-bombs and suffered severe damage.

An aerial view shows how present-day Munich has been restored retaining its medieval plan, with tightly packed buildings surrounding a central crossroads.

plans to reconstruct the Marienplatz. More than 360 sets of plans were submitted for consideration; 3,353 specialists and interested parties cast ballots indicating their choices. Most of the votes were for a plan to reconstruct the square exactly as it had been.

The same policy dictated the appearance today of another of Munich's finely designed squares: the grand and spacious Max-Joseph-Platz, which takes its name from Bavaria's first King, Maximilian Joseph, who ruled at the beginning of the 19th Century. The square is overlooked by the long south façade of the Residenz—the main palace of the Wittelsbach family, who ruled Bavaria for more than seven centuries. At right angles to the palace, forming the adjacent side of the square, is the much-loved and internationally famous opera house, the National Theatre; originally built in 1818, it was left in ruins after the war. Construction began, on a priority basis, in 1948 on a small new theatre to be incorporated within the Residenz building; but, during the ceremony held to mark the start of work, a small fir tree appeared at the top of the ruins of the National Theatre, for which there were still no rebuilding plans, with a sign made of flowers saying, *"Und ich?"* (What about me?).

Another 15 years were to pass before the National Theatre could open its doors to the public. The town council had at first decided to tear down the ruin and eventually build a new, modern opera house and theatre on the site. When the plans were announced in 1954 there was a storm of popular protest. The telephone switchboard was blocked for days on end with calls from irate citizens whose sensitivities were bruised by the very idea of scrapping the old National Theatre and building in its place a bland, smooth-faced, concrete and glass box. In the end, the city fathers were obliged to reverse their decision. The National Theatre was restored to its early 19th-Century splendour and the opening, on November 21, 1963, was a gala occasion.

As a result of the policy of careful restoration, Munich today looks much like its ancient self, with beautifully kept historic buildings on every hand—medieval, baroque, rococo, neoclassical. It is impossible to understand the special character of this trim, bright, comfortable city without bearing in mind that a significant proportion of the traditional buildings are actually no more than a few decades old. This realization imparts a slight oddness of focus to the city that is only resolved when you realize that many of the monuments, although perfectly authentic in their re-created form, lack the worn look that only the passage of time can bestow.

The rebuilding process continued by degrees throughout the 1950s and 1960s, with the curious side-effect that, as more old buildings reappeared, the city seemed to be aging again. Indeed, some buildings have been restored to a form pre-dating the one destroyed in the war. The Alter Hof or Old Castle, for example—the original fortress of the Wittelsbachs and one of Munich's oldest edifices—was rebuilt without various additions to

A Münchner shops at one of the vegetable stalls.

Provisioning a City

A fixture of the Munich scene since 1807, the city-centre Viktualienmarkt, located near the Marienplatz, was modernized in 1972 and is now brightened up with a beer garden, trees, flowers and fountains.

Early each morning it comes alive as stallholders arrive to unload their vehicles packed with flowers, fruit, vegetables, meat and cheeses from the Bavarian countryside. The women stallholders, who customarily pass their holdings from mother to daughter, combine shrewd business sense with an earthy good humour. The high point of their year is Shrove Tuesday, when they mark the end of Fasching with exuberant dancing in the square to the music of brass bands.

Contrasting with a skyline of spires in the old city, the colourful awnings of modern market stalls cover the paved area of the Viktualienmarkt.

its medieval core that had been made during the 19th Century. All in all, galleries and museums have been carefully restored and there are now few reminders of the war's catastrophic effects.

But some do exist. The 19th-Century Siegestor, or Victory Arch, the ceremonial northern entry on to the broad Ludwigstrasse that leads to the Residenz, has been left incompletely restored; it bears a plaque recording that its damaged state is a memorial to the ravages of war. A still more eloquent testimony is left by the shell of the erstwhile Bavarian Army Museum, a still-stately domed building that stands starkly on the eastern flank of the Hofgarten, a small formal park lying to the north of the Residenz.

Most of the vast sums of money required for the immense task of restoration were provided by the state and city governments, but some private owners also made contributions. Across the square from the Frauenkirche, one family restaurant that had been completely destroyed in the war claims with obvious pride on a sign above the entrance that, over a period of 25 years from 1949 to 1974, it had been faithfully rebuilt by the owners themselves in the original style.

In addition, prizes go to occupants of old buildings who restore their façades. Indeed, one of the most immediately striking impressions one receives in the city centre today is of block after block painted in the city's traditional pastel colours—ochre, pistachio, cream-yellow and duck-egg blue; the variations of paint serve to pick out the separate fronts of the spick-and-span buildings.

In the course of numerous postwar visits as a civilian in the 1950s and 1960s, I learnt more about the real Munich. It was a good period to do so. Over those years, the ancient city gradually acquired a new veneer: the addition of modern buildings, expanding industries and motorways that testify to the city's still-burgeoning economy. For the newcomer, it is necessary to penetrate this overlay if the underlying character of the city is to be observed and understood.

One thing that I found vital to this appreciation was a grasp of what it means to be a Bavarian. Quite simply, Bavarians take it for granted that they are "the best". They *know* it in the same way that Scots or Texans *know* it. Like Scotland, Bavaria was for centuries an autonomous country. It was first a duchy and eventually a kingdom, with a history spanning more than a thousand years. Though recognizing its dependence on the rest of West Germany, it has a unique stature, Texan in quality, that comes in part from its sheer size. Measuring almost 30,000 square miles, it is the biggest state in either West or East Germany. Bavarians talk in superlatives: their mountains are Germany's highest, their beer the best, their music the lustiest, their accent the most distinctive, their festivals the most uproarious and their football team, Bayern München, the most consistently successful.

Münchners are sustained by the feeling that their city, as well as their

Relaxing on a grassy bank, sunbathers while away a Saturday afternoon in the calm of the English Garden, north of the city centre. The spacious 18th-Century park, traversed by tributaries of the River Isar, is a haven for city-dwellers, with children's playgrounds and facilities for boating and swimming.

state, is without peer. It boasts world-famous collections of paintings and antiquities, Germany's largest library and largest university, the world's biggest museum of science and technology, and an internationally acclaimed group of film-makers. It combines—uniquely in present-day Germany—cultural strength with economic strength.

Munich is the third-largest West German city, its population of 1.3 million surpassed only by Hamburg's and West Berlin's. The city has its network of freeways, soaring over bridges and diving through underpasses, in inner and outer rings that act as hubs for the high-speed autobahns that reach out to other cities. It is also the third-largest industrial city in West Germany. Its rapid growth in the 1950s and 1960s, in both population and production, owes much to the transfer into it of people and investment, especially from Berlin, as a result of the postwar partition of Germany. So much of Berlin's role did Munich inherit that, when the news magazine *Der Spiegel* published an article on Munich in 1964, it dubbed the city "Germany's secret capital". The catch-phrase stuck and soon became a routine way of describing Munich's special role.

But underneath the surface of wealth and bustling industry is a subtler essence, the most fundamental qualities of which, it seems to me, are the ways in which the city is affected by its geographical position. Munich is set right in the centre of Europe and there is, in addition, a close interaction between the town and the countryside immediately surrounding it. The city reflects these two distinctive facets in its culture, in the character of its people—indeed, in its very feel.

January: skating on the ice in the English Garden.

February: revellers at the theatre during Fasching.

March: Strong Beer Time at the Salvator beer-cell

July: thirsty drinkers in the Hofbräuhaus courtyard.

August: country visitors take coffee at a farmhouse.

September: families return from summer holida

A Pleasure-Filled Year

With its packed calendar of festivals, fairs and traditional pastimes, Munich has the air of a city on permanent holiday. These evocative drawings in ink and watercolour, executed by the artist L. Bechstein in 1908, show the typical events of each month in early 20th-Century Munich, most of them still enjoyed today. The festive year begins with the carnival of Fasching on January 7, and continues in a whirl of celebration and activity. Spring is the season of strong beer and market fairs; summer brings boating, open-air balls and holidays in the country; and autumn is marked by the great Oktoberfest. After the opening of the hunting season, the year is seen out with family gatherings and firework displays.

: Easter egg-knocking in the Viktualienmarkt.

May: troubadours and guests at the artists' festival.

June: summer idyll by a lake in the English Garden.

ber: prizes for livestock at the Oktoberfest.

November: hunters out with their dachshunds.

December: ringing in the New Year with punch.

Munich is the pivot on the east-west axis between Paris and Vienna, and on the north-south axis between Berlin and Rome. To northerners, it is the first city of the south; and to southerners, the first city of the north—to all, a delightful point of transition, where lifelong dreams of distant journeys suddenly promise to be fulfilled. The signposts at the city's major road junctions foreshorten the geography of Europe. I can never see the sign for the autobahn to Salzburg, only 70 miles away on the Austrian border, without feeling an anticipatory thrill; for beyond the baroque jewel of Salzburg lies Venice, scarcely five hours away from Munich by car, or an overnight ride on the train. To the east stands Vienna, now no longer the centre of a widespread empire but a city at the eastern extremity of Western Europe. Beyond Vienna lies the Iron Curtain—Budapest and Prague. To the north-west of Munich is the Black Forest and beyond, nestling on the far side of the Rhine, is the French cathedral city of Strasbourg.

Being so far south, Munich was in the past always one of the first cities of Europe to feel new winds of thought and style coming from Italy. Both the 16th-Century Jesuit Michaelskirche and the 17th-Century Theatinerkirche—the beautiful Italianate church opposite the Residenz that was built by the Elector Ferdinand Maria to celebrate the birth of an heir in 1663—attest to the readiness with which Munich adopted the baroque style that was later naturalized into a characteristic South German form.

Even Greece, shimmering in the middle distance of the northerner's imagination, is adumbrated in the neoclassical architecture of a number of Munich's 19th-Century buildings, such as the original National Theatre and the Glyptothek sculpture gallery, erected by the city's philhellene Wittelsbach rulers. A Wittelsbach prince—Otto, son of Ludwig I—even became King of Greece when that country at last escaped in 1832 from subjection to the Ottoman Empire.

Munich is infused not only with the cultures of north and south, but also with the countryside in which it is set. One of its special delights is the River Isar, which draws its icy waters from the Austrian Alps only 30 miles away, and speeds through the Bavarian landscape in a light-green rush of water over a bed of sand and silver-white pebbles. Being so near its mountain source, the river is too shallow for navigation and thus remains free from industrial pollution. The waters are of startling clarity—as refreshing, as bracing to the sight as to the touch. Munich accommodates its river in a succession of styles: in one section a series of huge, shallow concrete steps soften the river's fall, and in another the Isar is allowed to keep its natural banks, with a park on one side and an esplanade on a natural rise along the other. Here, near the very heart of a large city, you can find fishermen in high rubber boots fly-casting in midstream.

North-east of the city centre, in Munich's spacious English Garden—an 18th-Century landscaped park about double the size of Hyde Park in London—the Isar suddenly loses its single-mindedness and runs

Their lunches wrapped in handkerchiefs according to rural custom, Upper Bavarians parade down the Ludwigstrasse in the Oktoberfest costume procession.

playful riot through the broad river-meadows in a network of diversionary streams where mallard ducks ride the gentle rapids. Rusticity is preserved and resurgent. The racing speed of the water is enough to remind you that it has come freshly from somewhere steep. The Isar, crisp and bright, brings into the city the feel of the nearby great mountains, even in winter when mist and clouds so often wrap them into invisibility.

That Munich can retain the atmosphere of a country town owes something also to the fact that the unhurried pace of the countryside has been deliberately built into the most recent fabric of the growing city. In 1972, for example, the year the Olympic Games were held in Munich, a large part of the old central area was banned to all private motor traffic and converted into a mainly pedestrianized zone. Unlike some similar districts elsewhere, the zone—large as it is—is easily accessible; in the central Marienplatz is the broad but unobtrusive access to a *U-bahn* station—a link in the metro system that, in 1971, was installed as part of the improvements stimulated by the impending Olympics. Delivered to the very middle of the area, people whose ears have been accustomed to the din of traffic gratefully re-attune themselves to the quieter sounds of voices and footsteps. Water gently splashes in the square's fountain; and perhaps the strains of a small band mingle with the voice of one of the many buskers; while, occasionally, a bell-like tone can be heard as a city tram warns of its approach.

This central area is especially popular in the summertime when it is blooming with flowers, but, to me, it is just as attractive in winter when clusters of people, pausing at the stalls that sell roasted chestnuts or heaped-up tangerines, form an almost medieval scene.

A consequence of the interaction of town and countryside is that Munich retains something of a village atmosphere. Not for nothing was it referred to until recently as the *Millionendorf*, the village of a million people. The traditional qualities of its inhabitants—indeed of the inhabitants of Bavaria as a whole—make nonsense of most clichéd preconceptions about what Germans are like. The differences between the North Germans and the South Germans are extensive and ill-defined, but they are freely acknowledged to exist and are even proudly claimed, especially by Bavarians from the country's heartland in the mountainous south, who consider themselves Bavarians first and Germans second.

Instead of being stolid, Protestant conformists, the inhabitants of southern (Upper) Bavaria are predominantly Catholic, relaxed and individualistic. They share with their neighbours, the Austrians, many traditions and characteristics, both social and cultural—from their natural gaiety and the similarity of accent to their devout Catholicism. In north and east Germany—especially in Prussia—tenant farmers with few rights toiled until the 19th Century on the vast estates of warlike nobles; by contrast, most of the peasants of Upper Bavaria, and the farmers of the agricultural lands to the

Part of a 25-acre area in the centre of old Munich that was developed as a pedestrian zone in 1972, the Marienplatz provides city-dwellers with a relaxed atmosphere in which to stroll, shop and take refreshment. Brightly dotted with painted kiosks and tubs of flowers, it is a favourite meeting-place for Münchners of all ages.

north in Lower Bavaria, have a long history of independence. Under the Wittelsbachs, they were free, landowning subjects who, on the whole, regarded their rulers affectionately, until their last king abdicated in 1918.

Munich has always been a "country town". There is a tradition of close contact and mutual respect between the urban population and the country residents. The ruler used to spend the winter in the city, occupying the Residenz, but the summer would send him and his family to one of their palaces in the surrounding countryside. Artists, drawn by the beauties of the rural scenery, were also a familiar presence among the country people and, at least from the early 19th Century, various writers, many of them city-dwellers, have brought a knowledge and understanding of the country's communities back to Munich. Whenever I go into a bookshop in Munich, I am struck by the number of customers leafing through books in the section marked "Bavarica"—a category covering everything from food and drink to poetry, folklore and treatises on history and architecture.

As you might expect, Munich has its village carnivals, even if they are on a scale befitting a *Millionendorf*. An American journalist, James P. O'Donnell, once wrote of a conversation he had with a Viennese friend:

"If all the world dreams about Vienna," O'Donnell asked, "what city do you Viennese dream about, when the mood is on?"

"If the mood is beauty," came the reply, "we dream of Paris. Paris has everything except the Alps. If the mood is beautiful women, we dream of Budapest . . . But if the mood is just plain *Gaudi*, fun for the fun of it, we don't have to dream. We can take the overnight express to Munich."

That answer is just as true today. No fewer than 116 days a year are set aside by the city elders of Munich for festivals, feasts and observances of one kind or another. These include Bavaria's 14 official holidays (more than in any other region of Germany), plus a whole succession of carousals that have evolved during Bavaria's 400 years of beer-producing history.

All Munich's festivals run on beer; it is the city's life-blood. Bavarians *know* that their beer is the best in the world. The city's unofficial anthem runs *"In München steht ein Hofbräuhaus—eins, zwei, gsuffa!"* (In Munich stands a court brewery—one, two, and down it goes!) and Bavarians have all the pride of a people who practically invented the drink; in the 16th Century, one of their rulers became the first to lay down official guidelines for proper brewing. Rightly, therefore, beer spans all classes. It is the common man's drink, but may also be the Bavarian equivalent of a snob wine.

I won't give you a consumer guide to Munich's beers—whole books have been written on the subject—but will content myself by telling you that there are basically two kinds of beer: the original dark, malty, full-bodied, sweetish *Dunkles*, served at room temperature, and the more recent, paler *Helles*, which is served chilled. But there are a score of varieties of increasing strengths, from *Märzenbier*, with an alcoholic content by volume averaging 5.5 per cent, to a whole series of brews that signify their extra punch with the ending *"—ator"* on their names. The world's strongest beer is *Kulminator*; boasting a prodigious 13.2 per cent alcohol, it is brewed in Kulmbach in northern Bavaria.

I said beer was the city's life-blood and that's no idle metaphor. It flows through the heart of Bavarian politics as well as its social life, as is shown by the very phrase a "beer-hall politician": a demagogue who appeals to the masses. The beer-halls are Munich's largest meeting-places; and they were used by politicians of all persuasions for years before the Nazis gave them such an infamous connotation. The trend started in the 1890s, when technical advances in the industry compelled breweries to merge and abandon their traditional, small installations in the centre of the city for vast, cost-efficient factories in the suburbs and the countryside. Doing so meant that large premises in the centre were left vacant, and the breweries wisely saw that these could be valuable outlets for their own products. Rapidly, the original sites were converted into outsized pubs that can, in some cases, hold as many as 5,000 people at a time.

So important is beer to the citizens of Munich that there are festivals, such as Strong Beer Time in March and Bock Beer Time in May, that exist solely to promote the consumption—on an enormous scale—of special brews. The biggest of all the festivals, simply because it lasts so long, is Fasching, as the national New-Year carnival is called in southern Germany. Fasching is the carousal to end all carousals—or would be if this were not Munich. It is the German Catholic panacea, a ritual revelry to enliven the deadly months of January and February. It begins on Twelfth Night, by

Dressed in Bavarian folk costume, known as "Tracht", two young men at a local festival in the suburb of Haidhausen make a striking contrast with a lass garbed in distinctly modern clothes. The man on the right is wearing formal Tracht, with black leather knee-breeches, but without the waistcoat or short jacket that should also be worn. The fellow on the left is outfitted in a more casual, everyday version of the costume: he has combined an ordinary shirt with rough leather shorts, traditional ankle-less socks and a Tracht hat, decorated with a brush of chamois hairs.

tradition in the artists' quarter of Schwabing, and ends only on Ash Wednesday about six weeks later, by which time it has involved the whole city.

During this period, everyone has a ball or, more usually, several. There are well over a hundred official Fasching events, offering a wide choice: the Chrysanthemum Ball, the Press Ball, the Munich Laundresses' Ball, the Pretzel-Makers' Ball, the Butchers' Ball, the Policemen's Fasching Ball, the Milkmaids' Ball. The great majority are masquerades with a premium on the exotic and the bizarre. (One Pied Piper of Hamelin became the talk of the town when it was discovered that the dead rats hanging by their tails from various points on his costume were real.) In addition, many Munich families play host to at least one Fasching party during the season.

During Fasching a man or a woman can escape for a while, forget himself or herself for weeks on end, play a new part in another life—in short, live the masquerade. Moral lapse is not just tolerated, it is encouraged. For a purpose, the Church adopted or incorporated the pagan rites that make up Fasching: the provision of a grand relief from everyday life. Fasching is ceremonial group therapy run wild.

A highlight of the carnival is the dance of the women on Shrove Tuesday at the Viktualienmarkt (Food Market). Here the ladies of the market—elderly butcher women, greengrocers and fishmongers, masked and garishly costumed and ever so slightly drunk—do a burlesque of Fasching. Dancing a bacchanal in a witches' chorus amid overturned cases, baskets and barrels throughout the market, they swing salted herrings over their heads and into the crowd, chant bawdy songs and stick bright feathers into the rumps of plucked geese and chickens. "Be careful you don't fall!", I once heard a spectator cry to a crone who was being particularly acrobatic on top of a huge barrel. "I cannot fall any further," cackled the grandmother in reply. "I am long since a fallen woman!"

Predictably, Munich also hosts the greatest beer festival in the world, the annual Oktoberfest—16 days of carousal, of drinking, overeating, singing, dancing, country-fair amusements, unbridled revelry, drunken scuffling and downright mayhem.

The Oktoberfest was born in 1810, on the occasion of the marriage between Crown Prince Ludwig—the future Ludwig I, perhaps Munich's most important ruler—and a Saxon princess, Therese von Sachsen-Hildburghausen. It was suggested that a horse-race should be held to celebrate the nuptials; and the race was so popular that the King decided it should be held every year. The racecourse was built in a vast meadow on the city's south-western outskirts and, in honour of the new Crown Princess, it was named *Theresienwiese*—Therese's Meadow.

Within a few years, farmers had added an agricultural show at which they entered their prize bulls in competitions. Eventually the horse-race itself was abandoned, the whole meadow being taken over by tents, sideshows and the milling crowds. As was the custom among Bavarians, a special beer, *Märzenbier*, was brewed annually for the occasion and, when people complained that the drink in their mugs was constantly being watered down by early snowfalls and autumn rains, the opening date was brought forward to accommodate them. Hence the fact that the Oktoberfest now begins in late September.

The festivities are presided over by a huge statue representing Bavaria. The 60-foot-high goddess—clad in a vaguely classical toga with an animal skin cinched round on top, and carrying a laurel wreath—stands on a prominence at the side of the meadow. She was poured in brass by the caster, Ferdinand von Miller, on the orders of King Ludwig I. Though Ludwig was a lover of the arts and set Munich squarely on the path of becoming a place devoted to them, it is universally conceded that "Bavaria" is not a work of art. To me, at least, she looks like Mae West in a bearskin.

The wreath she bears was for the victors, I concluded, since the Oktoberfest inevitably evolved quite quickly into a marathon of contests to determine who could drink the most draught beer (at Munich festivals the beer is sold only on tap), eat the most barbecued chicken or sausages or, for waitresses, who could carry the greatest number of *Masskrüge*—heavy beer mugs each holding a litre of ale.

This honour once belonged to Rosa of the Bräurösl beer tent who was able to carry 21 full *Masskrüge* at a time. This gives a very good idea of the general dimensions of typical Munich beer-hall waitresses. "It is amazing that anything so big can move so fast!" I heard one Oktoberfest patron observe. And an Irish-American journalist once apostrophized these waitresses as "flat-footed ballerinas of beer"—a reference both to their comfortable flat footwear and their Bavarian dirndl skirts that make them look like members of a giants' *corps de ballet.*

Then, too, each Oktoberfest competes with its predecessors. Pertinent and impertinent statistics for each year are totted up and publicized as though the Oktoberfest were some sort of World Series. In one recent year, for instance, a total of some four million litres of beer and 500,000 barbecued chickens were consumed during the 16 days of the festival.

The sheer raw energy of the festival is staggering. On my first visit I can remember watching two young, rather small men doing their tipsy best to demolish one another with their bare fists when one of them, going into a clinch, looked at me balefully and said "Do you want to get in on this?" Now, I stand just under six-foot-four, and anyway I was holding a mug of beer in one hand and a sausage and bun in the other, and my mouth was full of all three. I remember wondering vaguely, as a purely practical matter, how I would go about accepting the invitation, and how each of us might come out of it if I took them seriously. The effects of the Oktoberfest beer had softened both fighters so much that they were quite unable to inflict any real damage even on each other. In the end I said nothing; and the brawlers, quite unperturbed by my lack of response, simply went on punching one another.

Present-day levels of violence notwithstanding, it is this improbable scene that has stuck in my mind, typifying what the Oktoberfest should be: a beery, zany, but harmless romp. For the Bavarians—in their unshakeable self-confidence, their conviction that their way of life is the best—possess the secret of a special wisdom: the importance of not being earnest.

A Fine Annual Orgy

Oktoberfest waitresses demonstrate how to carry up to eight litres of Wies'n beer at a time, in glass mugs marked with the brewery's traditional symbol.

Every autumn, Munich stages one of Europe's biggest and most rumbustious jamborees: the 16-day Oktoberfest. More than five million revellers crowd into the Theresienwiese—an extensive area just west of the city centre usually called simply the Wies'n (meadows)—to enjoy the fairground amusements and to indulge in an orgy of eating and drinking. Six local breweries erect temporary wooden buildings known as beer "tents", each able to seat as many as 6,000 people; within them, an average of 500,000 roast chickens and 40 whole spit-roasted oxen are devoured each year. But the greatest attraction of the festival is its beer. The Märzenbier brew that is served at the Oktoberfest is known for the occasion as Wies'n beer and, over the course of the carousal, more than a million gallons of it are consumed by men, women and children.

AUGUSTINERBRÄU
W·GAST
AUTOMATIC-SKOOTER
CAFE KONDITOREI
KASSE

Visitors in their thousands throng the central avenue (left) that runs northwards through the Oktoberfest's 75-acre site towards the Paulskirche in the distance. Among the many attractions they can sample is a shooting gallery (inset) where customers aim at—and sometimes succeed in winning—posies of plastic flowers.

Knives and forks at the ready, two carvers prepare to serve hungry festival-goers with slices from a 700-pound spit-roasted ox it has taken nine hours to cook.

To a background of drinking-songs from a 30-piece band, thousands of revellers enjoy refreshment in one of the beer tents that stay open 12 hours a day.

Over a snack of pretzels at a beer-garden table, two matrons boisterously toast each other in Wies'n beer. The beer gardens, operated by Munich's breweries and restaurants, offer customers a slightly less noisy alternative to the crowded, stuffy interiors of the beer tents.

A boy drowses over his unfinished litre. Children may, by law, drink beer freely if they are with an adult.

Reacting to the effects of strong brew and bright sunlight, a solitary celebrant pauses in a corner of a beer garden before resuming his merry-making.

On a convenient patch of grass, a visitor to the festival surrenders to exhaustion and the toll of many beers by stretching out for a late afternoon nap.

2

Lasting Imprint of a Dynasty

The imposing façade of the National Theatre rises behind the bronze figure of the patron who commissioned it: Bavaria's first King, Max I Joseph, whose statue looks down benevolently on the square that bears his name. The original theatre, erected in 1818, was destroyed by fire; but by 1825, when Max died, it had been rebuilt with the addition of the distinctive upper gable.

The history of Munich is essentially the history of one ruling family, the Wittelsbachs. For more than 700 years—which makes them one of Europe's longest-lasting dynasties—they fought for Munich, commissioned the architects who built it and sponsored the artists who enriched it. The shape of today's city, with its palaces, squares, avenues and gardens, is largely their achievement—a royal capital laid out century by century to do justice to the presence of its rulers. Their generally beneficent rule lasted from 1180, when a Wittelsbach first became Duke of Bavaria, until 1918, when the old Europe was swept away after the First World War; and even then, although deposed from rule, the family continued—and continues—to occupy a special place in Bavaria.

Only the first 24 years of Munich's existence owed nothing at all to the Wittelsbachs. Bavaria in the 12th Century was just one of 1,800 ill-assorted German states and principalities that came within the orbit of the empire established by the great Frankish King Charlemagne 350 years before. This multiple entity eventually became known as the Holy Roman Empire of the German Nation, a name that throws a specious cloak of unity over a peculiarly diverse phenomenon. It was based upon an uneasy collaboration between the elected German ruler and the Pope in Rome. Even in Germany, the hold of the emperor over his vassal lords was shifting and tenuous; while in Italy, despite coronation by the Pope, he never enjoyed effective political control at all.

Munich owes its foundation to a series of those shifting allegiances that constantly tore and re-wove the imperial fabric. In the 1150s, the awesome Emperor Frederick I—Barbarossa (Red Beard) as the Italians called him—was attempting to knit his divided provinces together. He even invaded Italy briefly in the first of numerous vain attempts to bring its northern and central states under his control, an ambitious policy that resulted in more than a century of conflict between Germany and the Pope. One of his supporters in that adventure was a cousin, Henry the Lion, Duke of Saxony. As a reward for Henry's services, Barbarossa enlarged his sway by granting him the Duchy of Bavaria, one of the more important elements in the patchwork of the empire. It was a large and prosperous state with long-established cities, such as Augsburg and the capital Regensburg (both of which had been Roman colonies), and monasteries that were centres of learning.

Henry at once set about making his new state pay its way. He noted that one vital commodity—salt—passed through Bavaria on its way north from the salt-rich Alpine foothills around Salzburg (Salt Town), 72 miles to the south-east. The traders crossed the River Isar by bridge at the village of Upper Föhring (now a northern suburb of Munich) where they were charged a toll. The tolls went straight into the pocket of the powerful Bishop Otto of the neighbouring town of Freising. Under the empire, bishops wielded secular as well as spiritual power, and Otto happened to be Barbarossa's uncle. Henry decided to break the Bishop's monopoly. In 1158, he attacked Upper Föhring, burnt the bridge, destroyed the fortifications and built another bridge a couple of miles upstream to the south. Thereafter, the salt revenues came to him. Or at least most of them did: two years later, responding to Bishop Otto's protest at Henry's action, Barbarossa wisely decreed that his uncle should continue to be paid one-third of the receipts in compensation.

The place Henry chose for his new bridge was marked only by a small settlement of Benedictine monks, and it was usually referred to simply as *Munichen* or *zu den Mönchen*—"at the monks'".

Henry's good fortune did not last. In 1174, Barbarossa embarked on yet another disastrous Italian campaign; this time, Henry refused to help. In 1180, when the Emperor had recovered from his setback, he stripped his cousin of his titles and lands and replaced him with a more loyal subject who had served in Italy with distinction. The new Duke was Otto von Wittelsbach, a member of an old Bavarian noble family; and with Otto's appearance on the scene, the story of the dynasty begins.

At first, Munich's growth from a small trading settlement was steady but not dramatic. In 1255, Duke Ludwig the Stern first made it his family's residence, and in the early 14th Century, under Ludwig the Bavarian—the first of two Wittelsbachs who became Holy Roman Emperors—the town received solid new fortifications. But the Wittelsbach lands were progressively divided between competing heirs. By 1378, Bavaria was partitioned between three grandsons of the Emperor Ludwig, and feuding among the princely families disturbed the life of the country. It was not until 1505 that Bavaria was reunited under one duke and Munich—by now a heavily fortified town about one mile square—became the capital.

Little remains in Munich to recall the early days. Part of the city's oldest church, the Peterskirche, built in 1181, still exists, although the building has been much remodelled. A portion of the first ducal residence, the forbiddingly austere Alter Hof, survives as a reminder that the first Wittelsbachs needed their residence as much for defence against an independent townsfolk or feuding relatives of their own as for a palace. The ancient city walls have gone, but the sweeping boulevard that surrounds the inner city reflects their original line; three of the six gates—the Isartor, Sendlinger Tor and Karlstor—still stand, giving their names to present-day squares.

To understand Munich's medieval development thoroughly would be a lifetime's work. But, from the shadows of these centuries, from the feuds and alliances of kaleidoscopic complexity that constantly reshaped

Colourful 16th-Century scenes spring to mechanical life every morning in Munich's Marienplatz, when the Glockenspiel on the façade of the neo-Gothic New Town Hall strikes 11 o'clock. The activity of the upper platform re-creates the two-week-long feast held in 1568 to celebrate the wedding of Duke Wilhelm V and Renata of Lorraine, with the royal couple being entertained by folk dancers and some jousting knights. In the lower section, painted copper figures re-enact a dance, first performed by Munich's coopers during the plague of 1515-17 to cheer the spirits of their fellow-citizens.

Bavaria, one or two incidents and personalities emerge that seem to me to say something special about the city and the way it has evolved.

Take, for example, the origins of the enormous Frauenkirche—the Church of Our Lady—which was built entirely by the townspeople, without ducal or aristocratic backing. From the 13th Century onwards, an increasingly substantial class of burgesses was growing up in German cities. In Munich, perhaps because they were inspired by the magnificence of such wealthy trading cities as Landshut and Ingolstadt, the solid citizens banded together to create a cathedral that would do justice to their city and themselves: a church of the people, not of the princes. The enterprise was financed by collections from the city's 13,000 inhabitants, and by the sale of indulgences by churchmen.

Work started in 1468. It was a sound piece of planning. Worthy, massive, unimaginative and relatively cheap (the city fathers approved the use of red brick to avoid importing expensive stone), it had one over-riding quality: size. It was 325 feet long and its towers were as high. Over the centuries it has acquired a mass of decoration, but originally there was hardly any—no flying buttresses, no swirling tracery, no florid sculpture. Amazingly quickly, therefore, in just 20 years, the cathedral was almost complete. Only the steeples, victims of a tight budget, remained unfinished. They were given their copper cupolas in the early 1500s.

Despite the growing prosperity of its citizens and its position of political significance, Munich remained small, overshadowed by cities lying to the north, on the great trade routes overland from Venice to central Europe and France. Augsburg, with 50,000 inhabitants the largest of Germany's cities in 1500, and Nuremberg, with 30,000, both far outranked Munich's population of 13,500. And, although Munich's armourers and goldsmiths had a good reputation, the city did not boast any of the medieval industries (such as linen production) that swelled the population and coffers of the other centres. Nevertheless, it soon became known for an industry that ever since has been central to its economic and social well-being: brewing.

For centuries, Bavaria had been famous for its wines but, during the 13th and 14th Centuries, the region, along with the rest of Europe, began to undergo increasingly harsh winters—the beginning of what is now known as the "Little Ice Age" that ended during the 19th Century. Grape harvests suffered, and beer, which depended on the hardier crops of barley and hops, grew in importance.

A document in the Bavarian State Library's rich archives shows the significance that was soon attached to beer: it is the Purity Decree *(Reinheitsgebot)* issued by Duke Wilhelm IV in 1516 to control the ingredients in Bavarian beer. Such a ruling had been in force in Munich for more than 50 years, and the Duke decided to cash in on the growing national industry by formalizing the manufacture of beer throughout the state—and, of course, taxing the end-product. Beer was henceforth to consist of nothing but "barley, hops and water". Later, the regulation was amended to allow for beers made with other grains as well; in its amended form it was eventually applied to the whole of Germany—and it is still in force.

The rulers of Munich kept an interest in this profitable business: not only were they assured of a regular income through the taxation of private breweries, but they went into business themselves. In 1589 they established in the Alter Hof the original Court Brewery which was moved in 1644 to new premises—the Hafbräuhaus, which is still a beer-hall today.

Munich owes to the Wittelsbachs the beginnings of another of its main claims to fame: its collections of antiquities and works of art. The same Duke Wilhelm who issued the Purity Decree commissioned many paintings by leading artists of the day, mainly on subjects from ancient history and the Bible. But it was Wilhelm's son, Duke Albrecht V, who, besides making Munich one of the music capitals of Europe by his lavish spending on the court orchestra, laid the real foundation for the Wittelsbachs' unique art collections. Albrecht's acquisitions of paintings, tapestries, books and maps—added to by later rulers—have become the basis and core of Bavaria's extraordinarily rich state collections. In the Residenz, the palace that superseded the Alter Hof, he built a long vaulted gallery, known as the Antiquarium, for his Greek and Roman statues and other relics beloved of Renaissance Humanists.

No account of Munich can omit the Thirty Years' War, a mass of interlinked wars over religion, territory and dynastic successions that embroiled all of central Europe between 1618 and 1648. For Munich, the struggle brought, firstly, devastation, as it did for most regions of Germany. Secondly, it underscored the significance of Catholicism in the city's history. And thirdly, it threw up one of the greatest of the Wittelsbachs: Maximilian I.

For a century, Germany had been torn between the Catholics and those who upheld the Protestant doctrines of Martin Luther, first promulgated in the early 16th Century. The religion of the dissenters was strongest among the princes and peoples of northern Germany and the Scandinavian countries. Munich's position in the deep south, which had brought it so fruitfully within the ambit of Renaissance influences from Italy, also confirmed its staunch Catholicism. It was therefore fitting that one of Catholicism's greatest champions should emerge in Munich. Maximilian I was the first leader of the Catholic League formed in 1609 to combat the Protestant Union. At first he triumphed, sweeping east and north to capture Prague and Heidelberg. The North German princes, the Dutch and the Danes met with little success against him. The Swedes, however, succeeded, and under their King, Gustavus Adolphus, they occupied Munich in 1632, while Maximilian withdrew temporarily to Regensburg.

For the next 16 years, Protestant and Catholic armies wheeled back and forth across southern Germany. Munich changed hands five times more

The Little Monk

The *Münchner Kindl*, the motif of a child dressed in a monk's habit that is part of the city's coat of arms, can be found all over Munich. The symbol of the monk, which recalls the city's origins in an 8th-Century monastic settlement, has had many different forms. Its first known use was on a 13th-Century town seal, showing a cowled head under an arch of the town gate. Since the 17th Century, the figure has often been that of a child holding a Bible in one hand and extending the other in blessing.

Shown on these two pages are various examples of the *Münchner Kindl*. In its traditional form the motif appears on a stained-glass window in the Frauenkirche (top row, left); on a wooden plate (middle row, left); and above the main entrance of the New Town Hall (bottom row, centre). But also popular are more secular versions, in which a monk carries the Bavarian specialities of a beer mug and a radish: on a wooden butter press (middle row, second from left) and on carousel decorations for the city's annual Oktoberfest, complete with Hofbräuhaus beer mug (bottom row, left).

Münchner Kindl

before the war ended in 1648, and the effects were everywhere catastrophic. With rival armies living off the land, robbing and burning, Bavaria was reduced to a wasteland. In Munich, a victim of both war and plague, the population of 22,000 shrank by a third. In the city and all round, commerce and agriculture lay in ruins.

But when peace came at last in 1648, Bavaria began the task of recovery with its ruling family and religion unchanged. Maximilian was the only ruler involved in the Thirty Years' War to live right through the hostilities; indeed, he emerged more powerful than at the start. In 1623, as a condition of his support for the Habsburg Emperor, he had gained the territory of the Upper Palatinate and the accompanying status of Elector (the Electors in the Holy Roman Empire were those bishops or princes who held the privilege of a vote in the appointment of a new emperor). Thenceforth, the Bavarian ruler was known as Kurfürst (Elector) instead of Herzog (Duke).

One of Maximilian's chief contributions visible in Munich today was the superb Renaissance grandeur of the main imperial palace, the Residenz, which he had remodelled in the years immediately preceding the Thirty Years' War. In detail, the history of this building would be as complex as Bavaria's own, for each ruler added his own stamp to it, and over the centuries the character of the Residenz gradually changed from a fortress to a rambling group of courtyards and buildings. It was Maximilian who turned it into a unity, a palace unrivalled by that of any other German prince of the time. Under his direction there rose the 200-yard-long wing that fronts the Residenzstrasse. And behind this great west façade lay a number of courtyards, including the Kaiserhof, almost a hundred yards square. Arcades and passages link this court in the north-west corner of the Residenz with the site of the original Gothic castle to the east, thus imposing a grand design on an architectural jumble.

In its day, it was an acknowledged wonder, and remains so now. When Gustavus Adolphus of Sweden took up temporary residence there after his victory in 1632, he asked in amazement who had been responsible for the design of this masterpiece; he was told by Bavarian officials that Maximilian had conceived the whole thing himself. Since the name of no one presiding architectural genius has come down to us, Maximilian may indeed have been his own architect, creating for the first time a palace that truly reflected Wittelsbach power. As an Italian writer remarked in 1644, it was "more an emperor's than a duke's residence".

The end of the Thirty Years' War was not, of course, the end of war. Bavaria was still only one among 300 semi-independent German states—and there were, in addition, another 1,500 minor territories controlled directly by the Emperor. This political cauldron constantly seethed with disputes over land and succession, the relationship between the Bavarian Wittelsbachs and the Austrian Habsburgs continuing to be particularly stormy. Owing to its central position in the heart of the empire, Bavaria

Centuries of Rugged Independence

A.D. 777	**First recorded reference made to "Munichen" (at the monks'), small monastic settlement on the site of modern Munich**
903	**Precious salt shipments, bound northwards from the Salzburg region, cross River Isar over bridge at Upper Föhring, village just north of present-day Munich; powerful Bishop of Freising derives income from taxes levied on them**
1156	**Henry the Lion, Duke of Saxony, made Duke of Bavaria by Emperor Frederick Barbarossa, ruler of Holy Roman Empire encompassing most of central Europe**
1158	**Henry destroys Föhring toll bridge and builds his own at "Munichen", an action sanctioned by the Emperor; Munich is thus founded**
1175	**Town's first defensive walls built to enclose area of about 30 acres**
1180	**Henry is deposed after refusing to campaign in Italy with the Emperor; Duchy of Bavaria passes to Otto von Wittelsbach, founder of dynasty that lasts until 1918. Town's population estimated at one thousand**
1253	**Work starts on Alter Hof, first Wittelsbach castle**
1294	**City charter granted by Duke Rudolph of Bavaria**
1301-15	**Ludwig the Bavarian, German King and later Holy Roman Emperor, builds second wall around enlarged town, now three-quarters of a mile across; new wall marks Munich's boundaries for almost 500 years**
1468	**Work begins on the Frauenkirche, greatest of Munich's medieval Catholic churches, built largely with funds raised by townspeople**
1474	**Altes Rathaus (Old Town Hall), classic example of Gothic architecture, completed in city centre**
1550	**Under patronage of Duke Albrecht V, Munich begins to acquire reputation as city devoted to the arts**
1570	**Construction of Residenz palace, new home of the Wittelsbachs, begins just inside northern wall; over the following centuries, palace is enlarged and renovated many times**
1583-97	**Building of Michaelskirche, west of city centre, gives powerful expression to Munich's Catholicism and exemplifies Italian architectural influence**
1618	**Thirty Years' War breaks out between Catholic and Protestant factions in Europe; Munich deeply involved as Catholic stronghold**
1623	**As reward for supporting the Habsburg Emperor during Thirty Years' War, Dukes of Bavaria are made hereditary Electors, with privilege of voting for Holy Roman Emperor**
1632-34	**Swedes under King Gustavus Adolphus occupy Munich; city suffers devastating effects of war and plague. Population drops from 22,000 to 15,000**
1648	**Treaty of Westphalia ends Thirty Years' War**
1663	**Under Elector Ferdinand Maria, building of Theatinerkirche in north of city begins, marking high point of Bavarian baroque period**
1701	**War of Spanish Succession begins; Bavaria joins France against Germany, Austria-Hungary, Netherlands and Britain. Under Elector Max II Emanuel, Nymphenburg Palace in western Munich, begun in 1664, extended in French style**
1704	**Franco-Bavarian army defeated by Austrians and British at Blenheim; Max Emanuel flees to 10-year exile in France; Austrians annex Bavaria and occupy Munich until end of war in 1714**
1751-53	**Court theatre added to Residenz; later named after its architect François Cuvilliés, it becomes an outstanding example of rococo architecture**
1789	**American administrator Benjamin Thompson, named Count Rumford by Elector Karl Theodor for his services, begins creation of the landscaped English Garden along banks of the Isar**
1806	**Elector Max IV Joseph, after making separate peace with France during Napoleonic Wars, created King Maximilian I of Bavaria by Napoleon**

1810	First Oktoberfest, which becomes annual festival, marks marriage of Crown Prince Ludwig to Princess Therese von Sachsen-Hildburghausen
1811-18	Massive National Theatre, located on Max-Joseph-Platz in city centre, built in neoclassical style
1825	Ludwig I, planner of present-day Munich, ascends throne; during his reign, new suburbs are built to the north and west, more than doubling city's size. With royal patronage, Munich becomes brilliant centre of art and learning
1826-30	Alte Pinakothek, masterpiece of neoclassical architecture, and among the world's most important art galleries, built near Königsplatz in city's north-west sector
1848	Political unrest in Munich, in part over powerful influence on King Ludwig I of his mistress, dancer and adventuress Lola Montez, leads to abdication in favour of his son, Max II
1864	Ludwig II invites composer Richard Wagner to Munich and close friendship develops; one year later, first performance of "Tristan and Isolde" is held in National Theatre
1871	Bavaria joins German Empire, but retains many features of sovereign state, including its royal family
1886	Ludwig II declared insane; dies in mysterious circumstances
1893	Thomas Mann arrives in Munich; remains until 1933, when he goes into exile
1896	Publication of "Jugend" and "Simplicissimus", epoch-making artistic and satirical magazines, reinforces Munich's worldwide reputation for originality in the arts
1901	"Die Elf Scharfrichter", first of several cabarets specializing in political and social comment, opens in artists' district of Schwabing
1910	Population reaches 600,000
1912	Manifesto of the Blue Rider, a group linking international artists resident in Munich, contributes greatly to evolution of abstract art
1917	Russian Revolution during First World War provides inspiration for German socialists
1918	Berlin socialist Kurt Eisner leads revolution in Munich, forcing flight of Ludwig III and ending Wittelsbach monarchy
1919	Eisner killed by lone assassin. Bavaria's two short-lived soviet republics, under nominal control of Marxist intellectuals, involve country in brief civil war
1920	First meeting of newly formed Nazi Party held in Munich's Hofbräuhaus
1923	Adolf Hitler, leader of Nazi Party, launches abortive putsch from the Bürgerbräukeller with ultimate intention of seizing political control of city as a base for national revolution
1924	Hitler tried and imprisoned for eight months
1933	Hitler becomes German Chancellor in Berlin
1935	Hitler names city capital of Nazi movement
1938	Munich agreement reached; Britain, France and Italy agree to Germany's occupation of predominantly German-speaking Sudeten areas of Czechoslovakia
1939	Second World War declared. Bomb attempt on Hitler's life in Bürgerbräukeller fails
1940	Munich suffers first of 71 heavy wartime air raids, which ultimately destroy 60 per cent of city's public buildings and 30 per cent of private housing
1943	White Rose anti-Nazi student resistance movement, centred in Munich, crushed
1945	American 7th Army reaches city. Second World War ends. Munich boom begins with movement of industries and flight of refugees from Berlin and Eastern Zone to West German cities
1958	Reconstructed Cuvilliés Theatre, destroyed during war, opens. Population passes one million
1963	National Theatre, gutted in wartime raids, reopens
1970s	"New Wave" of young film-makers adds new dimension to city's reputation for artistic innovation
1972	Olympic Games cap Munich's status as a "world city"

acted as a buffer zone between the rival powers of Austria to the south and Prussia to the north. To protect their country's independence, the rulers of Bavaria were forced to tread a political tightrope—at times allying themselves to Austria, at times to France and at times to Prussia.

But through all these horrendous complexities two remarkable personalities stand out. One was a Wittelsbach Bavarian, Maximilian II Emanuel (whose name, like those of the other Maximilians of Munich's history, is usually shortened—without any disrespect—to Max). And the other, surprisingly, was an American: Benjamin Thompson, Count Rumford, an extraordinarily talented man who designed Munich's English Garden and revolutionized the city's society.

Max Emanuel was a fiery, egotistical and ambitious little warrior, Bavaria's answer (so he thought) to France's Louis XIV, the Sun King. Max created a new army for Bavaria and, in 1683, allied himself to the Habsburg Emperor Leopold. Ostensibly this was to combat a new menace from the East—the Turks—but in fact Max wanted for political reasons to marry Leopold's daughter, Maria Antonia. Though she was a woman of legendary ugliness, Maria Antonia had one enormous redeeming virtue: as the only daughter of Leopold and Margarita Teresa of Spain, she was claimant to the Spanish throne. When Vienna was assailed by the Turks, Max therefore sprang to Leopold's defence. Clad in his blue armour, and himself leading his troops in foolhardy assaults, he relieved Vienna, pursued the Turks south-eastwards through Hungary and finally defeated them in 1688 at Belgrade. Leopold, in gratitude, granted his desire: Max married Maria Antonia, but his hopes of securing the throne of Spain for his descendants were later dashed when their son died in infancy.

Maximilian returned in triumph to Munich after the victory of Belgrade with an army of Turkish prisoners to provide forced labour on road and construction work (their presence is recalled today by names like Türkenstrasse and Türkenkaserne). Confident that one day he would be chosen Holy Roman Emperor (he never was), Max was eager to build with a pomp and splendour that would rival Louis XIV's Versailles.

He therefore commissioned work on two palaces simultaneously, one at Nymphenburg, which had already been begun by his father Ferdinand Maria, the other at the village of Schleissheim, nine miles north of the city, near one which his grandfather had begun. Nymphenburg is an acknowledged success; although perhaps a modest place by Max's own grandiose standards, it was a dignified summer residence, conveniently close, at five miles west of the Residenz, for Max and his successors. But Schleissheim Castle was another story, and its fate reflects Max's own. His dreams of military greatness, of imperial glory, of architectural magnificence all eventually came to nought.

In keeping with the imperial status he hoped to achieve, Max planned Schleissheim Castle at enormous expense but scarcely had work on the

Seventeen arches span the 226-feet length of the Antiquarium, built in the Residenz in 1571 to house Albrecht V's collection of antiquities. The gallery was

converted at the end of that century into a banqueting hall by Wilhelm V, who commissioned the allegorical and landscape frescos on the walls and ceiling.

ambitious plans begun when the War of the Spanish Succession broke out. Defeated by Marlborough at the head of an Anglo-Austrian army at Blenheim in 1704, Max fled to France for 10 years, leaving Bavaria in the hands of the English and Austrians.

When he returned after the war, he was still eager to fulfil his Schleissheim dream, imbued as he now was even more deeply with visions of the white and gold baroque magnificence of Versailles. But all the various wars and other extravagances had so depleted the Bavarian treasury that the work proceeded only fitfully. When Max died in 1726 the building was still incomplete, and was not finished until the following year. Architecturally, its status is equivocal. The vast rooms, which nowadays echo to the stamp and chatter of tourists, seem soulless; but their very size, accentuated by huge paintings of the Turkish Wars, make the palace an imposing monument to Max's adventures in Eastern Europe.

No such equivocation is possible, however, when it comes to Schleissheim's crowning glory: its garden. The graceful walks, grassy rond-points and wooded canals remain to form a classic example of the formal French style of garden. Those gardens contrast strikingly with the informality of Munich's main park, the English Garden, to whose American designer, Count Rumford, the modern city owes a number of debts—as an account of his amazing career shows.

He was born Benjamin Thompson in Woburn, near Boston, Massachusetts, in 1753. By his teens he had shown himself a demanding, curious, self-disciplined and imaginative scholar. At 19, he was a schoolteacher in Rumford (present-day Concord), New Hampshire, and became a secret agent spying for the English on behalf of the Governor of New Hampshire. At the outbreak of the Revolutionary War, he fled to England carrying dispatches and, within a few years, still aged only 31, he was an Under-Secretary of State, and had been knighted for his services by George III. In addition, he had been made a member of the Royal Society, England's prestigious scientific institution, for his research into ballistics and firearms.

He set off in 1783 for Vienna, but while passing through Strasbourg he happened to meet a Bavarian prince named Maximilian Joseph who was a cousin of the reigning Bavarian Elector. The two hit it off, and Maximilian Joseph put Thompson in touch with the Elector Karl Theodor. In Munich, the Elector in turn offered Thompson a post as aide-de-camp and unofficial tutor to one of his illegitimate sons. Thompson readily accepted.

The American expatriate found Munich impoverished by fruitless wars and in a state of collapse. For one thing, Karl Theodor disliked the place. He came from a Mannheim branch of the Wittelsbach family and had had to leave his own beloved city to take on the rule of Bavaria, when the direct line of descent ended with the death of Elector Max III Joseph in 1777. Karl Theodor was roundly disliked in return by both the population and officials of the city. All of which did nothing to remedy the situation, and so

Munich suffered on and on. The aristocracy was debauched; there was no industry; the army was a hotbed of crime, indolence and corruption. Since military service was often imposed as a punishment, many of the soldiers were convicted criminals. Deserters terrorized the countryside or joined the city's thousands of beggars.

After four years of establishing himself at court, Thompson took his career in his hands and sent a detailed recommendation to Karl Theodor for turning the city's fortunes around. To Thompson's amazement, the Elector was delighted to have someone with some drive, and soon made him Minister of War, Head of the Police Department and Court Chamberlain, with extensive powers to improve life first for the army and then for the poverty-striken populace of Munich.

Thompson set to in a whirlwind of reforms. He established clean, comfortable garrisons for the soldiers. He introduced educational schemes for them and their families. He opened a cannon foundry, organized task forces to repair roads and drain marshes, ordered the garrisons to establish their own gardens, and even provided thoughtful advice on the benefits of a balanced diet and the rotation of crops.

Encouraged by the success of these plans, Thompson next turned his attention to the city's beggars. "To make vicious and abandoned people happy," he wrote later, "it has generally been supposed necessary *first* to make them virtuous. But why not reverse this order? *Why not make them first happy, and then virtuous*?" To this end he established a workshop in a disused factory with facilities for various crafts—carpentry, weaving, tanning—and a dining room and a kitchen. He even concocted a thick potato-and-barley soup still known today as *Rumfordsuppe.*

On the first day of the year 1790, Thompson rounded up most of the city's beggars—2,600 of them—and told them that if they made their way to his workshop they could work in warmth for food and money. Most accepted the offer. Within six years, the place was showing a good profit, and half the beggars had established themselves as regular members of the community. Moreover, they were grateful: when Thompson fell ill, hundreds of Munich's beggars gathered with other townsfolk to pray for him. "Imagine my feelings," he wrote, "public prayers for me!—for a private person!—a stranger!—a Protestant!"

But Thompson's lasting memorial is Munich's English Garden. North of the town lay a wild and marshy stretch, on the edges of which he took to training cadets. It occurred to him to turn this one square mile of wasteland into a public park, using the informal planting pioneered by the English landscape architect "Capability" Brown, in contrast to the geometric, formal French style of Versailles—and of the Schleissheim gardens.

With the Elector's permission, Thompson seconded a corps of the new Bavarian Army, paid them a bonus, clothed them in work uniforms made at his factory, and set them to draining the marshes. When the park was

As the market-place of old Munich—still the heart of today's city—the Marienplatz bustles with life in this 1760s scene. The view looks east towards the towered Old Town Hall (centre, background). The square is named after the statue of the Virgin (centre), erected by Max I in 1638 to commemorate the victims of plague and war. The wooden platforms (foreground) were used to display sacks of corn on market days.

opened to the public in 1793, it boasted rambling walks, sparkling streams and miniature waterfalls hidden among copses of beeches and limes—all carefully designed to seem as "natural" as possible. But the garden was to be useful, as well as decorative. In addition to a Chinese tower and a concert hall (the Rumfordsaal), there were farms where cattle could be bred, and cottages for the farm-hands to live in. Other attractions were soon added: a café and a boating lake that doubled as a skating area in winter. "Scarcely a city in the world," proclaimed an admiring American visitor, "can boast a finer park"; and that remains true today.

Thompson's success aroused vituperative jealousy in the city fathers, but he remained a hero both to the Elector and to the common people of Munich. In 1791, Karl Theodor made him a count of the Holy Roman Empire, and Thompson chose for his ennoblement the original name of the New Hampshire town he had left 25 years earlier—Rumford. The councillors' jealousies were, understandably, only made the more intense, and Karl Theodor, to avoid further embarrassment, acceded to Rumford's request to be made Ambassador in England. Rumford departed in 1798 for London. Though George III refused to accept one of his own knights as the representative of a foreign power, Rumford stayed to pursue a brilliant career in science, making notable contributions to the understanding of heat and friction. He never returned to Munich. In 1799 his friend and protector Karl Theodor died without a direct heir, to be succeeded by the Maximilian Joseph who, 16 years before, had first sent Rumford to Munich.

Max Joseph inherited a state in turmoil. Rumford's reforms, though dramatic and effective, were limited in scope: he had not touched the administration. The bureaucracy, the law, the finances, all needed attention. In particular, both rulers and ruled needed constitutional inoculation against the revolutionary fever that had gripped France and, under Napoleon's dynamic leadership, threatened to engulf all of Europe. Max's aim was to ensure Bavaria's independence and then to initiate much-needed internal reforms. He proved more than equal to the task.

First, to avoid involvement in the war, he made his own peace with Napoleon, for which he was made King, becoming Max I. Then, having also been rewarded with possession of the northern, Protestant areas of Franconia and Nuremberg, he abolished discrimination against Protestants. He liberalized the criminal code, devised a new Constitution with an upper and lower representative assembly to give the people a voice in government, and introduced elementary education. In brief, he laid the foundations of a new Bavaria. No wonder he was referred to as "Father Max".

In 1800, just as Max Joseph was beginning his reign, Munich was still a medieval city in appearance. The original 14th-Century walls hemmed in a mass of low-eaved houses that crowded over narrow streets. It still had a mere 40,000 inhabitants; yet fifty years later, it was a city of 100,000, and

An 18th-Century marble statue of the god Jupiter looks down on two young mortals as they race through the formal gardens behind the Nymphenburg Palace.

Glorious Nymphenburg

The magnificent buildings and 500-acre landscaped grounds of the Nymphenburg Palace, five miles west of Munich, are open to the public throughout the year. Formerly the summer residence of the ruling Wittelsbachs, the palace originated as a dairy farm —a gift from the Elector Ferdinand Maria to his wife on the first birthday of their son and heir in 1663. Under the direction of the Electress Adelaide the following year, a summer villa was built and adjacent Italian gardens laid out. Successive rulers added pavilions to the villa and remodelled the gardens according to the fashions of their time. Completed in the 1820s, the complex also contains a famous porcelain factory.

An aerial view dramatizes the symmetry of the Nymphenburg Palace's front park, laid out in the 18th Century, with its central canal, lawns and paths.

King Ludwig I stands surrounded by artists and scholars offering works of art in this 1848 painting. The Glyptothek (background) was constructed in 1816 to hold the Wittelsbach sculpture collection; it is one of the many buildings in the neoclassical style with which the King transformed the appearance of Munich.

had spread way beyond its ancient confines. The chief architect of this expansion, politically and architecturally, was King Ludwig I. The city, until the destruction of the Second World War, was virtually his creation.

Ludwig was a remarkable character. Born in Strasbourg in 1786, the son of King Max I, he grew up during the French Revolution and the Napoleonic Wars. Ludwig loathed the French, and conceived a correspondingly powerful vision of a strong Germany, not a single nation but a federation of states linked by a common culture. His own particular brand of nationalism was combined with a strong sense of practical Christian duty and a passion for the arts. He fervently believed that German artists could rival the achievements of classical times and of the Italian Renaissance.

The city and the state he inherited in 1825 provided a solid foundation for his plans. True, Bavaria was still largely a country of uneducated peasants, and there were crippling public debts, the heritage of his father Max's support of Napoleon in the wars. But Max's new Constitution had provided a working, if expensive, bureaucracy and the beginnings of universal education. On this foundation, Ludwig rapidly threw up the political and economic bulwarks of a modern kingdom. He imposed stringent cuts on the administration and the army. He decentralized the bureaucracy. He brought the kingdom's university, founded in 1472, to Munich, from its previous site at Landshut. He formed a tariff league with several other German states. He opened a canal connecting the Rhine to the Danube, and thus the North Sea to the Black Sea. To get through the volume of work he generated he set a formidable example for his staff: he was in his office at

4.30 a.m., his light alone shining out from the darkened Residenz; and his frugality was proverbial: he wore the same overcoat for decades.

For Munich, Ludwig wanted nothing less than pre-eminence. "No one will be able to say he knows Germany if he does not know Munich," he said. Within a few years, he was well on his way to achieving his aims. He laid out new suburbs to the north and west and, to give them a worthy focus, created the Königsplatz beyond the city walls to the north-west; spacious and grand, it is still Munich's most impressive square. An exuberant devotee of the various forms of classical architecture, Ludwig lined the square with glorious buildings in a variety of Greek styles—the Glyptothek (sculpture museum) in the Ionic style, the exhibition hall of the Antique Collections in the Corinthian style and the Propyläen, a vast marble entrance for the road going west, in the Doric style. Just around the corner, in the Barerstrasse, arose the Alte Pinakothek picture gallery in Italian Renaissance style.

Leading northwards from the Residenz, the King laid the broad Ludwigstrasse, building at its southern end a classical loggia known as the Feldherrnhalle; where the road ended in the north was raised the Siegestor, a tribute to Bavaria's past military glories.

To design, build and decorate his city, Ludwig I employed North German artists, turning—as befitted a dedicated nationalist—to German sources where previous rulers had brought architects from France and Italy.

Ludwig patronized all the arts, not just architecture. He often quoted Goethe's words: "We must do our utmost to encourage the Beautiful, because the Useful encourages itself." And he did so. Until Ludwig's accession it was said that Rome was the capital of German painting, but he encouraged many of the expatriates to settle and work in his own city, and Munich soon had no rival in all Germany as a *Kunststadt* (city of art).

Ludwig himself bought paintings and antiques by the ton. His collections form the core of the Alte Pinakothek, one of the great art museums of the Western world; the Neue Pinakothek, destroyed during the war, contained his 19th-Century pictures; the classical sculpture that he bought can still be seen in the Glyptothek and the Antique Collections. None of this he regarded as extravagant, an attitude he found hard to put over, complaining: "If you lose your money at the gambling tables or spend it on horses people approve and think that's how it should be. But if you spend it on art, they call it extravagance." No doubt he would be gratified to know that the collections, as prime tourist attractions, have paid for themselves many times over. The people of Munich are also indebted to Ludwig for another of their famous attractions, the Oktoberfest. His marriage in October 1810 to the Saxon Princess Therese von Sachsen-Hildburghausen, 15 years before his accession as King, was the occasion for the original celebrations that became an annual event.

But there were clouds on Ludwig's horizon, which ultimately brought about his downfall. His domineering Minister for Internal Affairs, Karl von

Created for Ludwig I in the early 19th Century, the broad Ludwigstrasse boulevard stretches northwards for three-quarters of a mile from central Munich to the triple-arched Siegestor (Victory Gate), modelled on Rome's Arch of Constantine. Severely damaged during the Second World War and deliberately left so, the gate now bears the inscription: "Dedicated to victory. Destroyed by war. A reminder of peace."

Abel, antagonized both the Protestants and the Catholics. There was also growing unrest among workers and students, which in 1848 (as elsewhere in Europe) broke into open revolt. And then, running through the rising discontent, was the problem of Ludwig's most notable mistress, the famous adventuress Lola Montez.

In spite of his ascetic regimen, the King had something of a weakness for women. His "Gallery of Beautiful Women", a series of paintings that he commissioned from the artist Joseph Stieler, constituted one of the great artistic attractions of the Residenz, and although historians insist that it was not a collection of his mistresses, it certainly includes several women who were. One of them was depicted by the court painter, Wilhelm von Kaulbach, as a harpy, whip in hand and belted with snakes. Her maiden name was Marie Dolores Eliza Rosanna Gilbert. But she was known throughout Europe by her stage name: Señora Maria de los Dolores Porris y Montez, or Lola Montez for short. Lola, said to be the daughter of an Irish soldier of fortune and a Spanish noblewoman, was born in Limerick, Ireland, in 1818 (at least, according to most accounts; she herself claimed that she was born in Seville). At the age of 19, she married an English lieutenant, divorced him, and went on the stage as a dancer. In 1843, she appeared in London, where she was seen to possess little talent as a dancer, but such beauty that she was kept fully booked.

In 1846, fleeing from France after a public scandal following the death of her lover in a duel, she arrived in Munich. The story goes that she insinuated herself into a private audience with Ludwig, then aged 60, whose experienced eye told him that Lola's curves were accentuated by hidden supports in her gown. When he voiced his suspicion, Lola produced a knife from behind her Spanish veil and, to the King's delighted amazement, slashed her dress to expose her bosom, thus proving him wrong.

This was the beginning of the end for Ludwig. Ignoring the pleas and warnings of his ministers, he wrote any number of effusive love letters and fulsome verses to Lola, calling her his "lovely Andalusian". He even promised to make her a countess. At this, the conservative Abel balked. He refused the government's consent, threatening to resign if Lola were granted the Bavarian citizenship necessary before she could be ennobled. Ludwig accepted his resignation and wrung the agreement he needed from Abel's successor; Lola became the Countess von Landsfeld.

The university sprang to Abel's defence. Professors denounced Ludwig and students marched to the countess's villa chanting in Latin *"Pereat! Pereat!"* (Let her perish!) Lola appeared on a balcony waving a pistol, which was taken from her by one of her companions. In its place, she seized a champagne bottle, drank disdainfully to the mob's health, and proceeded to pelt them with sweets.

In response to the ugly demonstration, Ludwig suspended all lectures at the university. At once, Lola became the symbol of misgovernment, and the students joined the rioting townspeople on the streets. The city—like so many others in Europe in that year of revolutions, 1848—seemed about to fall. Ludwig was left with no alternative: he made a smart about-turn, re-opened the university, and agreed to deport Lola. She fled for her life, her carriage pursued by an enraged crowd throwing stones, hats and canes. She ended up lecturing on beauty in America, where she died in 1861.

Ludwig was horrified by the anger of the mob and was utterly out of sympathy with the demands for a more democratic system. On March 20, 1848, he startled Bavaria and all Europe by abdicating in favour of his son, Maximilian II. Ludwig lived on for 20 years, some of the time in Munich, where he became once again a popular figure, the rest of the time in his beloved Italy, where in 1868 he died.

Under Max II, many of the liberal demands that had horrified Ludwig—such as those for electoral reform—were quietly conceded by the government, and in 16 years of relative calm Max brought to Munich a new reputation for scholarship and science.

Not that he ignored architecture; south of the Residenz he created an imposing avenue—the Maximilianstrasse—lined with neo-Gothic buildings and solid businessmen's houses. It leads over the Isar by the Maximilian Bridge to the vast Maximilianeum, a building originally intended as a suitable residence for young men of good family in the service of the State; it now houses the Bavarian State Parliament.

But for Max, building was not an end in itself; that had been Ludwig's forte. Instead, Max decided to concentrate on an area that had until then been neglected: the city's intellectual life. There was no tradition of writing, research and scholarship as there was in Berlin, Vienna, Paris and London. Max therefore invited writers and scientists from North Germany. Among the scores of thinkers he enticed to his frequent symposia, at which he encouraged discussions on a myriad of specialist topics, were Justus von Liebig, one of the fathers of modern chemistry, and the novelist and poet Paul Heyse, who later won the Nobel Prize for Literature.

Nor did Max ignore the arts, for which Munich had by now a European reputation. In Wilhelm von Kaulbach—who had painted Lola Montez—Ludwig I had created the first of a succession of painters so wealthy and influential that they came to be known as Munich's "painter-princes". During Max's reign, and later, in the last three decades of the 19th Century, two native Bavarians extended the importance of the painter-princes: the history painter Karl Piloty, who designed a series of murals for the Maximilianeum, and one of his pupils, the portraitist Franz Lenbach. Each in turn acquired a "von" upon being ennobled, and Lenbach was to become the best-known and most highly paid portrait-painter of his time. The list of those who sat for their portraits includes Pope Leo XIII, Ludwig II and his successor the Prince Regent, Kaiser Wilhelm I, Count Helmuth von Moltke (Bismarck's Chief of Staff) and Otto von Bismarck himself, the

Designed in the 1880s for the influential painter Franz Lenbach when he was at the height of his fame, this neo-Renaissance villa close to the Königsplatz testifies to the artist's wealth and success. In 1924 the residence, with its furnishings and collections, was acquired by the city, and today serves as a gallery entirely devoted to exhibitions of art created in Munich.

Kaiser's "Iron Chancellor", who became Lenbach's close friend, and of whom Lenbach made a whole series of studies.

Where other court portraitists painted their subjects' ribbons and decorations with almost too great an exactitude, Lenbach insisted on the starkest simplicity. Even the buttons on generals' uniforms were quietly omitted, possibly because he was so short-sighted that even with his thick glasses he could not make out such detail. Wilhelm I thought that he, at least, should be portrayed with a minimum of one decoration on his chest; Lenbach thought otherwise. When Wilhelm tried to insist, Lenbach pressed a brush into the startled Kaiser's hand, remarking: "Perhaps Your Majesty would prefer to paint in your own decoration!"

At the age of 51, Lenbach married the 24-year-old Countess von Moltke, General Moltke's niece, and built himself a large and sumptuous residence that came to be known simply as the Lenbachhaus. It now houses the city's Municipal Gallery, with its superb collection of paintings from the 19th and 20th Centuries. Here, in this vast neo-Renaissance villa, Lenbach, the painter-prince *par excellence*, lived surrounded by what one contemporary described as "a wreath of dazzlingly beautiful women", models whom he dressed and coiffured, and thus transformed into what were popularly known as "Lenbach beauties".

In the second half of the 19th Century, during the period of Lenbach's artistic ascendancy, Bavaria underwent an epoch-making political change, finally becoming part of a unified Germany. The King who presided over this momentous event, Ludwig II, was one of the century's most romantic and eccentric figures, who died in circumstances that, to this day, have never been satisfactorily explained.

Ludwig II came to the throne in 1864, when the Prussian Prime Minister, Bismarck, was already beginning the task of creating a unified German Empire that would be a successor to the original *Reich*. After Prussia's success in the war against France in 1871, Bismarck at last managed to persuade Ludwig and the other South German states to join his North German Confederation under Kaiser Wilhelm I. Although Bavaria retained its own ruling family and internal organization, over the next few years it steadily lost the rights of an autonomous, sovereign state; Bavarian laws were slowly replaced by imperial ones, for instance, and Bavaria's armed forces were to be commanded by a Prussian general staff in time of war. What Bavaria gained from all these changes was, of course, a new security and a voice in the counsels of Germany.

Being an accessory to this change in Bavaria's history would have cemented Ludwig's place in the story of Munich. But his claim to notoriety is for most people based on his personal predilection for castles and lodges in wild mountainous settings. His extravagant romanticism at first seemed mere self-indulgence. The earliest manifestation of this tendency was his patronage of the composer Richard Wagner, in whose musical genius the King found an imagination extravagant enough to match his own. Together this ill-assorted pair—Ludwig was 6′ 2″ tall and a mere teenager when they met, Wagner was a stocky 5′ 6″ and 32 years his senior—spun fantastic plans for a new world of music. But Ludwig's ministers and many others, distrusting Wagner's influence over the King, opposed their schemes and succeeded eventually in displacing the composer from court.

As the disappointed Ludwig grew older he gradually became more suspicious of his friends and family, convinced that he was surrounded by enemies. He began to avoid his capital in which he never did build anything of significance; a winter garden on top of the Residenz, established in 1867, proved so dangerously heavy that it had to be removed in 1897.

Ludwig devoted himself instead to the work of creating a fantasy world of castles, forfeiting by his prolonged absences from the city the popularity that his remarkable good looks had gained for him at the start of his reign. On a barely accessible cliff, 55 miles south-west of Munich, he began construction of the mock-medieval castle of Neuschwanstein. In the Ammer forest rose the florid Linderhof Palace in the style of a Louis XIV château. On an island in the Chiemsee, 42 miles to the east of Munich, he began to build an imitation of the Grand Trianon at Versailles. Like Neuschwanstein, it was never entirely completed; simultaneously he dreamt of yet more castles—one in the Gothic style, another in the Chinese—all testimony to the King's increasing eccentricity.

Though Ludwig's extravagances cost the State nothing—he financed his projects himself—his plans became more and more preposterously expensive, and to pay for them he concocted wild schemes to borrow money that proved a great embarrassment to the government. Eventually, no one had any doubt that he was out of touch with reality and, in 1886, a commission was appointed to pronounce him insane, and he was forthwith put under restraint. He was declared incompetent to rule, and his uncle, Prince Luitpold, was made Regent in his place.

Ludwig, who was only 41 years old, died three days after he was deprived of his liberty, in circumstances that at once became the subject of wild rumour. He was first driven to the 16th-Century Schloss Berg, for many years his favourite home, on the Starnberg Lake, 16 miles southwest of Munich. With him was the head of Upper Bavaria's lunatic asylum, Dr. Bernhard von Gudden. The first night in the castle was peaceful enough, and when the following evening Ludwig asked to go for a walk along the lakeside, Dr. von Gudden, presumably reassured by the ex-King's apparent calmness, agreed. The two set off together. Neither was seen alive again. At 11 p.m., the two bodies were found lying in shallow water near the shore, having died apparently after a struggle.

There have been many theories to explain this extraordinary event, none very satisfactory. Suicide, with Gudden attempting vainly to prevent it, is one possibility, but surely, rather implausible in shallow water? Perhaps the more likely—and even more dramatic—theory is that the King made a desperate, foolhardy attempt to escape by swimming the mile-wide lake. If Gudden attempted to stop him, and Ludwig fought back with his superior height and bulk, he could have succeeded in drowning the unfortunate doctor, only to succumb himself to a heart attack. The Wittelsbach family have never released the confidential report that was made of the investigation into the two deaths.

Ludwig's successor, the Prince Regent, was to rule over the whole of the *belle époque* until 1912, when he died at the age of 91. Luitpold, no less than his predecessors, was a patron of the arts and a lover of music, but times had changed. Luitpold could no longer *order* vast buildings at public expense. Bavaria was part of a massive empire, expenditure was carefully budgeted, and the focus of political interest was now Berlin. For the first time since the building of the Frauenkirche in the 14th Century, the city itself and private developers took over the role that had for so long been that of the Wittelsbachs, building huge structures like the Law Courts, the National Museum and the Science Museum.

With Luitpold's death, the days of the Wittelsbachs as a ruling dynasty were numbered. Luitpold's successor, Ludwig III, presided over the descent into the maelstrom of the First World War, and abdicated in 1918.

But there are still Wittelsbachs in Bavaria. Germany, I have heard it said, is good to its aristocrats, and certainly Bavaria has been generous in its arrangements with the Wittelsbachs. Although most of their enormous possessions, including the Munich Residenz, the castles at Schleissheim, Linderhof, Neuschwanstein and Herrenchiemsee, together with the priceless collections of valuables, went to the State, the smaller castles remained in the family and others again—Nymphenburg for example—were left available to the Wittelsbachs, who have the right of unlimited residence, although the public is admitted to the grounds and state apartments. In such ways does the modern Bavarian state still acknowledge the special status of the family whose fortunes have been closely bound up with the city's fortunes for so many centuries.

A City of Dog-Lovers

Members of Munich's Boxer Club talk earnestly against a background of show certificates and photographs. Boxers originated in Munich in the 1890s.

Munich is a city of dog-lovers; and its abundant parks, open spaces and paved pedestrian areas might have been designed with man's best friend particularly in mind. Whether strolling, shopping or taking refreshment in one of the city's cafés or beer gardens, a dog-owning Münchner is rarely seen without at least one four-legged companion in tow. Among the most popular breeds are dachshunds, poodles and boxers; but lap-dogs of any kind—pedigree or mongrel—are held in almost equal regard. Canine inhabitants of Munich have their material needs catered for by specialist shops; and some of them also receive the Church's blessing, a tradition dating back to the Middle Ages. On October 4, St. Francis' Day, Munich's animal-lovers lead their pets to the Holy Ghost Church, near the Marienplatz, where a special prayer is said.

An elderly lady embraces her beloved "Zamperl"—the pet name given by Münchners to any small lap-dog.

Under the admiring eyes of an onlooker in Munich's English Garden, a long-haired dachshund begs obediently for a reward from its doting mistress.

A pair of pugs receive affectionate cuddles from their owners during Sunday morning exercise in the landscaped gardens along the east bank of the Isar.

Two Münchners take their dachshunds on a leisurely stroll in the south-western suburbs. The smooth-haired breed, long popular among the city's dog-aficionados, became the official Olympic mascot when pictures of it appeared on souvenirs commemorating the 1972 Games.

Spruced up for St. Francis' Day, a couple show off their St. Bernard, who wears a traditional brandy barrel.

Elegant in a loden suit, a cloth made throughout the Alpine region, a Münchner sets off with her boxer in the pedestrianized city centre.

Silhouetted in the soft light of early morning, a man and his poodle take a solitary walk by the artificial lake in Olympic Park, north of central Munich.

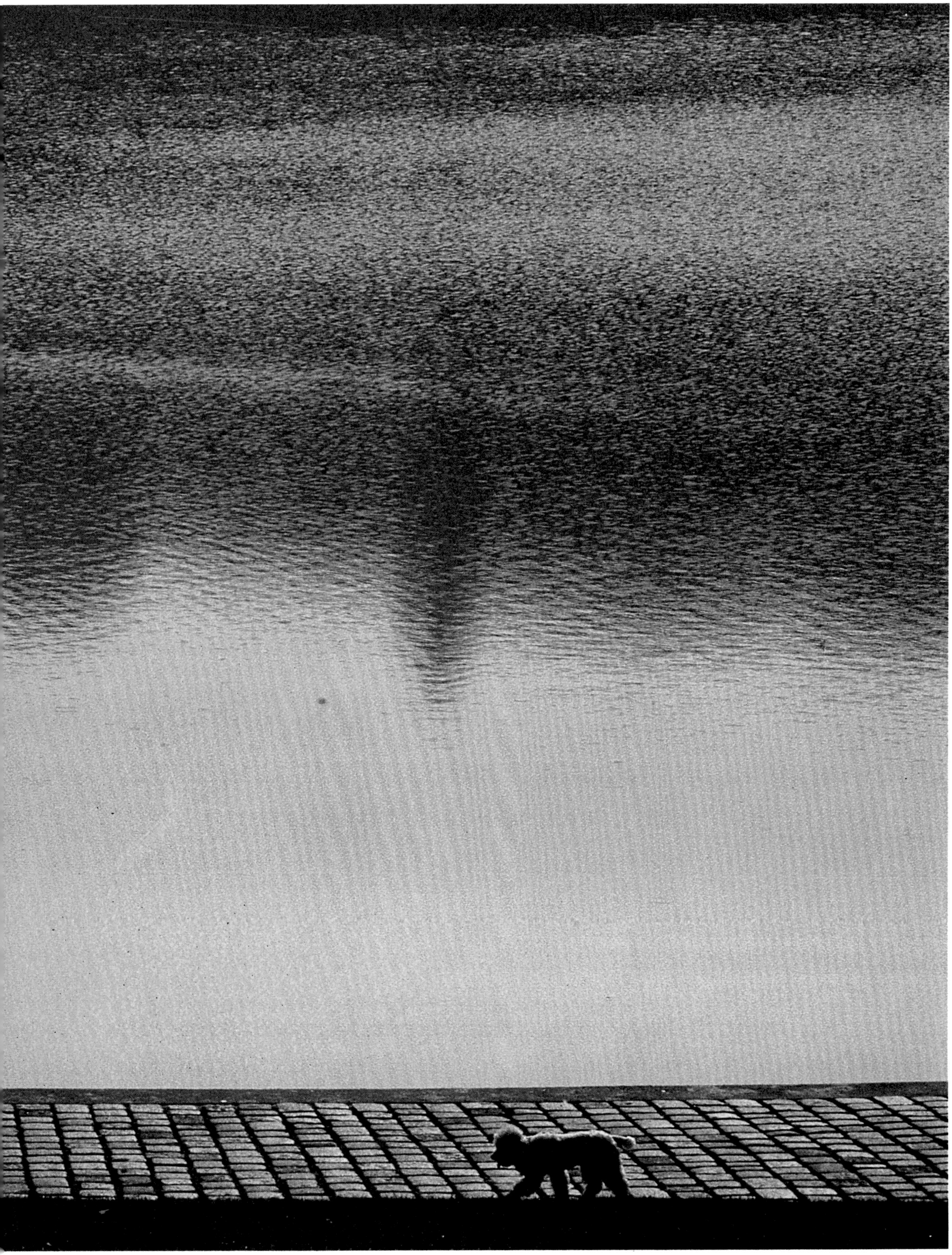

3

Music, Music, Music

Munich is an intensely musical city. The evidence of this public passion for music is everywhere. It can be seen in such lavishly subsidized official institutions as the National Theatre (home of the Bavarian State Opera), the operetta theatre, the opera festival held every year in summer; the Philharmonic Orchestra and the four other resident symphony and chamber orchestras; and it is manifest in the city's numerous amateur choruses, string quartets and other chamber music groups, the music schools and youth orchestras and the constant succession of concerts and recitals, many of them held in salons and halls of palaces and museums in and around the city. The quality of amateur music-making is extremely high, and the standard of professional performance is correspondingly exciting. It is backed up by a tradition that long ago established Munich as one of the great centres of European music.

One thing I have noticed in my experience with music in Munich is that it need not always be in deadly earnest; the city's vigorous Fasching tradition means that musicians, like everybody else, have always known how to have a good time. And the fact that people here like to amuse themselves is not a minor point, to be tucked away in a footnote: it has had a palpable influence on the forms and fashions of Munich music. The historian of Munich's Opera House, Alfons Ott, points out that when opera, that most theatrical form of musical entertainment, was first imported from Italy in the 17th Century, it was warmly welcomed by the Münchners because it corresponded to "that baroque love of life that led to so many manifestations of aesthetic sensuality and the lust for life in the whole of Bavaria". In consequence, opera took root more quickly and more thoroughly than in other parts of Germany, and was acclimatized to the point where it became an essential part of Munich public life. As Ott rightly points out, "it grew naturally out of the mentality of this land".

This mentality had expressed itself since the beginning of Bavarian history in the people's love of pageantry and make-believe, in the wearing of mummers' masks and elaborate disguises that marks Fasching, and in the great processions with which church festivals and the state occasions of the Wittelsbach court were celebrated. Musical life centred upon the court, where many musicians were employed as part of the household. Sacred and secular occasions equally provided those public spectacles in which the Münchners delighted. Folk happenings such as maruska (morris) dancing became court happenings and vice versa; the line between them was hard to draw. As long ago as the 15th and 16th Centuries, the

A rococo creation of glowing crimson and gold, the old theatre in the Residenz palace—known after its architect as the Cuvilliés Theatre—provides the perfect setting for the regular performance of baroque operas and classical plays. Built for Max III Joseph and his court, the theatre, faithfully restored, retains an intimate 18th-Century atmosphere.

masters of music at the Munich court set great store by the *Mummereien* (mummers' dances) and *Aufzüge* (processional compositions) with which they enlivened the ceremonials of the dukes of Bavaria.

The people of Munich danced, sang, strummed and fiddled while accompanying the triumphal carriages when Duke Wilhelm V celebrated his marriage to the Princess Renata of Lorraine in 1568, and the master of these revels was none other than Orlando di Lasso (also known as Rolandus Lassus), the Duke's *Hofkapellmeister* or musical director. A Fleming who had worked in Italy—and therefore combined the traditions of the two most important schools of the period—he was the first of a succession of great European composers to make their home in Munich. The "newspapers" of that day were written in rhyme, to be passed by word of mouth (since hardly anyone knew how to read), and one account of Duke Wilhelm's festivities had it that:

Der grosse Saal war vil zü eng
Die Stabelmaister alle vier
Mussten machen da Platz gar schier . . .

which I take to mean, in 16th-Century German doggerel, that so many people came to the palace that the large audience hall proved far too small, and the Duke's four chamberlains had to push and shove in order to clear a space for the musicians.

Audiences are just as keen today, it seems, and one has to be very much on the *qui vive* to snap up a ticket, especially for operatic performances. The opera is still the special pride of Munich, yet it is by no means a luxury confined to the rich and fashionable. Many Münchners take out subscription tickets for the Bavarian State Opera's season so that they are assured of a seat, and certain senior-ranking Bavarian civil servants also receive regular free tickets. The local audience is a well-informed and enthusiastic one, which also likes to do full justice to its own participation in the evening's theatrical performance: people always dress formally and elegantly.

The status of the theatre—and particularly of opera—in German cities owes much to the history of a country that was made up, until late in the 19th Century, of numerous small princely states. For their rulers, a fine court theatre offered the perfect setting where a prince or a duke could—besides amusing himself—be seen by his courtiers in beautifully arranged and stately surroundings.

Present-day Munich audiences, the inheritors of the Wittelsbach capital city, seem to welcome the opportunity to see and be seen with the same enthusiasm. On a summer evening in the Max-Joseph-Platz, when opera-goers drift out in the interval—champagne glasses in their hands—on to the broad steps of the National Theatre's portico, they are almost on stage themselves, overlooked by the imposing façade of the Residenz. Trams glide past and an occasional car circles the square to disappear down a ramp into a central underground car park; but right in the middle of the

A charming memorial tablet of red marble, set into one wall of the Frauenkirche, depicts the blind composer Konrad Paumann, who died in Munich in 1473. Around him are shown some of the instruments he played, including the lute, the harp, the flute and the portable organ. Famed as an organist, Paumann left his native Nuremberg for the Wittelsbach court and was a pioneer of German instrumental music.

everyday city, there is a feeling of celebration that reminds one that it was originally laid out with great occasions in mind.

During Munich's Festspiel season every July and August—when the main attraction is the international opera festival—the impression of elegance is heightened by the presence of opera-lovers from all over the world. The performances, some of which are staged by the Munich Opera and others by visiting companies, are by no means monopolized by the smart international visitors; the usual Munich audience mingles with the glittering throng, strolling across the square as is customary when the performance has ended to drink beer and eat dumpling soup at the Spätenbrau restaurant opposite.

The State Opera presents the grandest form of musical entertainment in Munich, but the Theater am Gärtnerplatz also provides delightful evenings of opera and operetta, from Mozart's lighter works to Lerner and Loewe musical comedies. On a flying visit to Munich one winter, I decided I did not want to leave the city without hearing some music. The National Theatre was sold out as usual, but—just ahead of a Chinese visitor and two music students—I managed to get the last *Stehplatz* (standing room) ticket for Mozart's *The Magic Flute* that night at the Gärtnerplatz Theatre. A standing room ticket does not mean that you have to stand the whole time: you have a comfortable brocade seat, but because it is in the back row at the side of the balcony, you cannot see the whole stage while sitting down. The production was not a new or fashionable one, but the performance was entertaining and good humoured, and the haunting solo flute passages, floating through the warm, darkened theatre from the invisible flautist below, sounded the equal of any playing I have heard. My evening was well and appropriately spent.

Munich may be richer than most cities in opportunities to hear classical works, but its musical life has many other faces too. For one thing, the national pride of Bavarians in their own culture and institutions has been heightened in recent decades by the presence of so many arrivals from other parts of Germany, eager to share in the special appeal of Bavaria; one of the results has been a keener interest in Bavarian folk music—that sweet (sometimes over-sweet), close-harmony, vocal music with a suggestion of yodelling in it that reminds you Bavaria is in part an Alpine land.

There is hardly a time when you can turn on the radio without finding a jolly or wistful folk song, or a zither-and-accordion folk dance, somewhere along the wave bands. At one end of the scale, the passion for Bavarian folk music can produce vulgar colour television spectaculars of jolly "peasants" singing up-dated songs, but at the other there is much scholarly investigation and preservation of a still-living tradition of music.

At the same time, Munich is one of the few European cities where jazz can be heard every night—often very good jazz indeed. The city receives a steady stream of internationally famous players and bands, and stages its own large-scale jazz festival in the summer, filling, without apparent difficulty, the 10,000 seats of the Olympic Hall.

If you don't want to go to one of Munich's numerous jazz clubs of an evening, perhaps you can drive out instead to the stately Schloss Schleissheim, one of the Wittelsbach palaces just outside Munich, and sit in the ornate Great Hall listening to the sinuous sounds of a visiting string quartet; or there may be a concert of baroque music in the Herkulessaal—a richly tapestried chamber in the Residenz—given by a serious-minded consort of players on scrupulously authentic contemporary instruments.

But if today the musical calendar is always crowded with events, the past was just as eventful. If you look back at what has happened here over the centuries you will see that many of the red-letter days of music history have taken place in Munich: the world premières of two of Mozart's operas, for example, and of several of Richard Wagner's, as well as an important part of the career of Richard Strauss, a native son who took the Munich spirit to the four corners of the musical world. It is these three—Mozart, Wagner, Strauss—whose heads, in bronze, are enshrined in the entrance hall of the National Theatre as patron saints of the local musical scene.

Mozart, for one, kept coming back to Munich hoping to find a job that would allow him to settle in these agreeable surroundings. "I like it here," he wrote to his father in 1777, when he was 21; and indeed the whole family had nothing but praise for the place. As a boy of six, Mozart had given a recital with his 10-year-old sister Nannerl for the Elector, Maximilian III Joseph, and, when they returned a year later, they were given a guided tour of all the palaces in and around Munich. Nannerl found it delightful and instructive to wander through the rococo splendour of her host's many residences: "Amalienburg is the most beautiful, it has the loveliest bed and a kitchen in which the Electress herself did the cooking. Badenburg is the largest, it has a salon full of mirrors and a bath made of marble. Bagodenburg [Pagodenburg] is the smallest and the walls are covered with majolica tiles."

Nannerl's brother returned to Munich at the age of 18, with a swollen jaw and a toothache, carrying the nearly finished score of his opera *La Finta Giardiniera*, which the Elector had specially commissioned for the Munich carnival of 1775. It proved to be a huge success and, as usual, the theatre was so packed that a lot of people had to be turned away at the door. "Then after each aria there was a terrific noise, clapping of hands and cries of 'Viva Maestro'," as Mozart proudly reported to his mother, who had stayed in Salzburg. The Electress and the Dowager Electress joined in the shouts of "Bravo!" and then, "I went off with Papa to a certain room through which the Elector and the whole court had to pass and I kissed the hands of the Elector and Electress and Their Highnesses, who were all very gracious."

But when Mozart returned to Munich two years later to ask the Elector

The royal families of Saxony and Poland are shown being entertained by their Wittelsbach relations at Nymphenburg in this 1761 painting by Peter Horemans, entitled "Conversation Piece". Max III Joseph joins at cards (right, foreground), while his wife, the Electress Maria Anna (far right) partakes of refreshments.

for a job as court composer and conductor, he met with disappointment. Max III, also known to his people as *der Gute* (the Good) or *der Vielgeliebte* (the Well-loved), was popular both for his economy measures, which included sharply reduced expenditures for court functionaries, and for his readiness to use his own fortune for the public good. Like any other office-seeker, Mozart had to wait in the Residenz for a propitious moment to approach His Highness—or rather, as Mozart was careful to address him, *Euer Kurfürstliche Durchlaucht*, a phrase which is difficult to translate in all its baroque allusiveness and orotundity. The usual translation is "Your Serene Highness", though it really means something more like "Your Electoral-Altogether-Steeped-in-Wisdom-ness" or "Your Electoral-Princely-Illuminatedness"—pronounced, of course, with an appropriately sweeping bow in the direction of the addressee.

History records the following conversation (here condensed from the account in Mozart's letters), which decided the young man's future, and deprived Munich of the chance to rival Vienna as a *Mozartstadt*.

Mozart: Will Your Serene Highness permit me to throw myself humbly at his feet and offer him my services?

Maximilian III Joseph: Yes, my dear boy, but I have no vacancy. I am sorry. If only there were a vacancy . . .

Mozart: I assure Your Serene Highness that I shall not fail to do credit to Munich.

Max III: I know. But it is no good, for there is no vacancy here.

Nothing daunted, Mozart was back again in 1780 to introduce another new opera, *Idomeneo*, at the court theatre. Max III had meanwhile gone to his heavenly rest but his successor, Karl Theodor, was on hand to watch the rehearsals. After the first act he shouted "Bravo!", and after the thunderstorm music at the beginning of the second he turned to the young composer and told him, with a laugh, "Who would believe that such great things could be hidden in so small a head?" Nonetheless, Mozart never succeeded in getting a job at the court. In 1781 he settled in Vienna where he eventually secured a post as chamber composer to the Austrian Emperor in 1787, but died four years later, deeply in debt.

If Mozart's ghost were to come back to the Residenz tomorrow to stage a revival of *Idomeneo*, he would find almost everything just the way he left it. The court theatre where Mozart played and conducted is one of the great architectural treasures of Munich—an 18th-Century opera house with its incredible wealth of imagery and ornamentation perfectly restored.

The little jewel, officially the Altes Residenztheater, is known colloquially as the Cuvilliés Theatre, after the architect who designed it, François de Cuvilliés the Elder. Born in 1695 in what is now Belgium, he was hired at the age of 11 by the Elector Max Emanuel, who spent part of his reign in exile from Munich at his court in the Spanish Netherlands. Cuvilliés was evidently of very small stature, for he is referred to in the court archives, as a dwarf. Indeed, he seems to have been hired originally for his appearance —dwarfs were fashionable curiosities at the time—but he quickly turned out to have marked talents for drawing and design. Cuvilliés went to Munich on the Elector's return to power in 1715 and was employed as a draughtsman in the Office of Works, where his skill encouraged his employers to send him to Paris for further training as an architect. He already had an impressive list of commissioned buildings to his name when he started to create the new court theatre in 1750 for Max III Joseph.

I find it a strangely moving experience to attend any sort of concert or operatic performance in this enchanted place. It is tucked away in the inner recesses of the Residenz; the way to it leads past the bronze lions that guard the side gates of the palace, through a cobbled courtyard and past a baroque fountain on which the figure of Otto, the first Wittelsbach Duke, is surrounded by mythological people and beasts, whose goat heads were already spouting bubbling streams of water a century before Mozart himself set foot on these stones.

Once inside the building one enters a sort of time-machine that instantly wafts one back to the world of the 18th Century. Cuvilliés had a marvellous sense of proportion. His horseshoe plan has four tiers of boxes that flank the magnificent royal (or rather, electoral) box, itself a piece of sculptural theatre *par excellence*. The box is two storeys high and lined with mirrors. The ruler's monogram "M.J." is emblazoned on a cartouche surmounted by a giant replica of the electoral crown; beside it a scantily clad figure of Fame blows silent fanfares through a slender, straight clarino trumpet.

One tier of boxes is supported by a row of caryatids and atlantes in polychromed wood; the rest are ornamented with bas-relief sculptures and symbolic heads—of figures such as Diana, goddess of the chase (her game bag, hunting horns, fowling piece and hunting knife are carved in relief on the balustrade below), Apollo, the god of poetry, Mercury, the god of commerce (who has served Munich so well in recent years), Bacchus, the god of wine (he was chosen, presumably, in the absence of a classical god of beer) and, transatlantic visitors please note, an American Indian girl, whose head is crowned with feathers, but in a style better known to courtly Versailles than to the Dakotas. With her attributes of a drum, a club, bows, arrows and a cactus, she symbolizes America, in a series devoted to the continents; Australia is missing because it was still unknown to Europeans at the time when the theatre was being built.

Sitting in one of the gilded and garlanded boxes, one feels enveloped by this great womb of a theatre. At the same time—and this is what most strikes me about the place—one is seized by a sense of community with the rest of the audience, a feeling of solidarity that I have never experienced in an ordinary theatre. The acoustics are an essential part of the theatre's character. The whole of Monsieur Cuvilliés' theatre acts as a giant sounding-board for the fragile timbres of the baroque: the velvet tones of

Cremona violins, the janizary twang of harpsichords, or the forest fanfares of the hunting horn. So this is how Mozart's music sounded in its native habitat, as opposed to the cavernous concert-hall sound we have become accustomed to: reverberant, mellow and yet hard-edged! It is worth a visit to Munich just to hear Mozart performed in his aural setting.

Periodically they do, in fact, stage his operas here, and then again the *cognoscenti* flock to the theatre until not another soul can be crammed into the parterre or the boxes (altogether there are only 456 seats), and the spirit of Mozart watches from the wings. I have noticed, too, that on such nights the women in the audience seem to take care to observe the dramatic unities, and dress in a style that is in character with the setting. Watteau *décolletés* and sweeping ballgowns prevail, so that the classical illusion, at once grand and intimate, is complete.

You may well wonder how it was possible, in this city so badly damaged by bombs, that Cuvilliés' fragile designs escaped destruction. It was not luck, in fact, but careful precautions that saved the theatre. In 1943, before the worst of the air raids hit Munich, all the ornaments and sculptures were dismantled and packed away out of harm's reach in places outside the city, many of them in the cellars of old castles. One of the curators told me that the carvings, when disassembled, came to 30,000 pieces! Six weeks after the interior was stripped and the theatre was re-opened with makeshift fittings, the Residenz was bombed and the Cuvilliés Theatre was wrecked along with the rest of the building.

After the war, the gutted walls were strengthened and a new, entirely modern theatre was built within them, the Neues Residenztheater. At that juncture there was neither the time nor the money for a complete historical restoration, and the panelling and decorations remained in their packing cases. Not until 1956 did the Bavarian Schlösserverwaltung—the office that administers the former royal palaces—address itself to the problem of what to do with Cuvilliés' legacy. Then, by a happy chance, the original layout was found to fit snugly into one of the unused wings of the Residenz, just around the corner from its former location. They rebuilt the entire theatre according to Cuvilliés' plans. The job of re-assembling the giant jig-saw was a daunting one and, in addition, some of the hastily stored pieces had suffered from damp and were beyond repair. But after two years of painstaking restoration, the theatre was completed, just in time to mark the 800th anniversary of the founding of Munich, celebrated in June 1958. For the inaugural performance, needless to add, they chose something by Mozart: *The Marriage of Figaro.*

In this resurrected theatre there was only one significant departure from the décor as Mozart knew it: electric lights had replaced the beeswax candles that lit the way for *Idomeneo*. Even so, the crystal chandeliers give a flickering, ghostly light as they are smoothly raised on long steel cables that pass through the ceiling, so as to be out of the line of sight when the

Gazing serenely from a Munich shop window, the busts of this wildly ill-assorted pair—Elvis ("the King") Presley and King Ludwig II of Bavaria—nevertheless make a point about the inclusiveness of the city's musical scene. The late demigod of rock and roll is revered by his many fans in Munich, while Ludwig is fondly remembered by appreciators of classical music as the friend and patron of Richard Wagner.

curtain rises. This, too, was a technique they used in Mozart's day—though the ropes were of hemp and the motive power human rather than electric.

Somehow this theatre is for me one of the quintessential symbols of the Munich spirit, and not only because it reflects the "aesthetic sensuality and the lust for life" that have always been part of the local scene, but because it is a piece of a great tradition that has survived—or rather, has been preserved and adapted—so that it can continue to serve a socially useful purpose in the modern world. This is Munich in a nutshell: innovation firmly wedded to tradition, the beautiful to the utilitarian.

The Residenz makes such a perfect setting for Mozart that most visitors overlook the fact that it also served as the backdrop for an even more dramatic episode in the city's musical history—the spectacular chapter involving Richard Wagner and King Ludwig II. The Munich Opera has always been famous for its Wagnerian productions and, if Munich can lay claim to Wagner as one of its local demigods, the credit for this belongs first and foremost to Ludwig and his extraordinary vision in matters touching on music and architecture.

In another age he might have been called Ludwig the Great. But, as luck would have it, he came to the throne in the 1860s just when his country was moving into the age of commerce and industry, and the situation demanded a public-relations-minded monarch, who could be depended on to cut ribbons at trade fairs and to lay cornerstones for banks. Ludwig, on the other hand, possessed a romantic imagination, and saw himself as a figure out of knightly legend. Nothing could have been more appropriate to his visions than the myth-making music-dramas of Richard Wagner, with their heroic tales of medieval chivalry. Ludwig had fallen in love with the stories of Wagner's early operas when a boy, acting out fairy-tales with his brother. As he afterwards told Wagner, "You were *the sole source of my delight* from my tenderest youth onwards".

When his father's sudden death in 1864 brought Ludwig to the throne at the age of 18, one of his first concerns was to send for this composer whose music he adored and whose writings on the mission of art he admired. At that crucial moment Wagner's fortunes happened to be at their lowest ebb. He had always had a hard time earning a living as a composer, but now, at 51, he had exhausted the patience of his creditors, several of whom had tried to have him arrested. He was, in fact, leading the life of a fugitive when Ludwig's emissary found him in Stuttgart. But Wagner's first meeting with the King, in the Munich Residenz on May 4, 1864, resolved all the composer's financial problems and established the pattern of their relationship from then on. Wagner wrote to a friend the next day that their interview had been "one great never-wanting-to-end love scene. He offers me everything I need to live, to create, to perform my works. I am only expected to be his friend: there is no job to hold, no service to perform. And that this should happen to me now—now, in the darkest night of my existence!"

Ludwig gave Wagner large sums of money to pay his debts and promised the composer that he would do everything in his power to make up to him what he had suffered in the past. Wagner moved into a private villa near the royal residence on Starnberg Lake and, later in the year, into a town house at Briennerstrasse 21, one of the main avenues leading to the Residenz. His gratitude was expressed in a *Huldigungsmarsch* or "homage march" known as the "Young King of Bavaria's March", which was first performed during a serenade in the courtyard of the Residenz, with selections from his operas *Tannhäuser* and *Lohengrin*. Music like this, Ludwig confessed, transported him into realms of "indescribable delights".

Together Ludwig and Wagner formulated elaborate plans for a great music centre that was to be established in Munich, and which was to include a festival theatre dedicated to Wagner's conception of the all-embracing work of art, the *Gesamtkunstwerk* that would combine music, words and theatrical spectacle into an indissoluble whole. "When we two have long been dead," Ludwig wrote to him, "our work will still be a shining example to distant posterity, a delight to the centuries; and hearts will glow with enthusiasm for art, the God-given, the eternally living!"

Ludwig saw to it that Wagner's earlier works received command performances at the Munich Opera House, which had been completed in 1818. But their real collaboration did not begin until the private performance of *Tristan and Isolde* given before Ludwig and 600 invited guests in May 1865. It could have taken place nowhere else, for the operatic world

The tenor Ludwig Schnorr von Carolsfeld and his soprano wife, Malvina, first to sing the roles of Tristan and Isolde, here re-create a poignant moment from Wagner's great opera for a studio portrait taken at the time of the 1865 première in Munich. Considered by the composer to be the best Wagnerian singer of his day, Schnorr died soon after his Tristan début, aged only 29.

was convinced that *Tristan* was an unsingable score. Because of its innovatory style and—for the period—huge orchestral forces, Wagner's music needed singers of phenomenal stamina and vocal range, who were also capable of acting and prepared to work hard at understanding the composer's unprecedented musical intentions. In Lucerne six years earlier, *Tristan* had already been abandoned as unperformable after 72 rehearsals. There was great hostility to Wagner in many quarters of the European music world, and it was only in Munich, thanks to Ludwig's championship, that he found the opportunity to make another attempt. He could also call upon the abilities and loyalty of the great tenor, Ludwig Schnorr von Carolsfeld, one of the few singers equal to the demands of the work.

Wagner, who was feeling unwell, left the conducting to his disciple Hans von Bülow, but before the curtain went up he stepped on stage, dressed completely in black, and apologized for not conducting himself. He asked his audience to join with him in an attempt to defeat the hatred of his musical opponents by offering love instead: "the means that Tristan and Isolde have taught us. With you it rests to achieve this magic of love."

In later years Wagner looked back on these *Tristan* days as some of the happiest of his life. Thanks to Ludwig he had proved to a doubting world that his latest music-drama was also the most powerful and melodic of his works. Both he and the King were confident that ultimately they would succeed in regenerating the world by means of Wagner's immense artistic programme. It was a dream of the romantic ideal to which both were wholly committed. They wrote effusive letters to each other—more than 600 of them—that take up the better part of five thick volumes published half a century after their deaths. The tone of these letters is dreamlike and rapturous, as befits a fairy-tale king and a composer of mythopoetic operas. Certainly no other king and no other composer had ever communicated with each other in such ecstatic terms.

Wagner to Ludwig: "My dearest beloved, my only, most magnificent friend. With tears in my eyes I ask: How are you? Are you sad? Are you happy? How does my most gracious king feel?

"Highest glory of my life, sun that shall light up my nights, redeemer, saviour of my existence! It is—wonderful—because it is more wonderful than a poet could imagine it.

"Yes! He found me.

"My adored friend! Could I ever part from him again?

"Now *Tristan* is being born, he grows, he flourishes; every day now brings us a feast—a feast of thanksgiving for you, King *Parsifal.*

"Loyally yours forever, Richard Wagner."

Ludwig to Wagner: "My dearly beloved and only friend!

"Soon I hope to see the beloved again!—I want to be joyful and glad for I have heard that you are happy; when I know that you are, then so am I!

"With deepest joy I have learnt that the rehearsals of *Tristan* are going well!—Oh how blessed will be the day of the first performance! The most beautiful hopes, the strongest yearnings of my soul have been fulfilled! Oh, I am yours in life, yours in death!

"Eternally, your Ludwig."

It was certainly a contrast to "Yes, my dear boy, but I have no vacancy."

The sense of these letters should not be misinterpreted. In the hot-house atmosphere of Ludwig's court, the King and composer adopted in their letters the elevated phrases of Wagner's libretto for *Tristan*. But, despite Ludwig's untiring support for Wagner's projects, their intended art revolution failed to come off, and the festival theatre that Ludwig hoped to build near his palace on the banks of the River Isar never became a reality —at least not in the environs of Munich.

This plan, in fact, together with Wagner's increasing financial demands and some attempts of his to interfere in politics, aroused a storm of criticism among Ludwig's advisors; ultimately their opposition forced Wagner to leave Munich. He and his household moved to the shores of Lake Lucerne in Switzerland—and the festival theatre was ultimately built, not in Ludwig's capital, but in Bayreuth, a small town 96 miles to the north, where sympathetic members of the town council welcomed the enterprise.

Yet the intimate connection between Munich and the works of Wagner was never really severed. Until the inauguration of the Bayreuth theatre in 1876, all the important Wagner world premières—*Die Meistersinger von Nürnberg, Das Rheingold, Die Walküre*—continued to take place at the Munich Opera. And, although it is the Bayreuth Festival that serves as the Mecca of the Wagnerian world, Bayreuth has always been heavily beholden to Munich for its singers, stage designers, and conductors; and many of the best productions of *Tristan, Die Meistersinger* and the *Ring* cycle were those first mounted by the Munich Opera. Many of the greatest Wagner conductors were active in Munich; among them Hermann Levi (who conducted the first *Parsifal*), Felix Mottl and Bruno Walter.

If Wagner's ghost were to take his cue from Mozart's and come back to the Munich Opera tomorrow to stage a revival of *Tristan*, he too would find nearly everything just the way he left it. Built in 1818, destroyed during the Second World War and rebuilt in 1963, the National Theatre is still one of the world's most beautiful opera houses, and its acoustics are precisely right for romantic opera, from *Fidelio* to *Madame Butterfly*.

It is just a stone's throw from the Cuvilliés Theatre and, although it is four times larger than its neighbour (seating 2,049), there is a definite family resemblance. The clean, uncluttered lines of early 19th-Century Empire classicism have replaced the exuberance of rococo, and yet this is still, palpably, a royal opera house, with the monarch's box in the dominant central position, flanked by two huge and pneumatic caryatids who look like lifeguards from some empire of Amazons. The Bavarian coat of arms is emblazoned on the balustrade in a far more subdued and classical setting

The Bavarian State Opera rehearses a frenzied scene from Act Three of "Der Rosenkavalier", composed in 1911 by native Münchner Richard Strauss.

than one finds in the Residenz next door. More than sixty years after the abdication of the last of the Wittelsbachs, people still refer to it, of course, as the *Königsloge* (the king's box) and indeed on special occasions it is still reserved for visiting heads of state, including the odd king or queen.

I sat in it once myself, when I was part of an international group of journalists who were being shown the sights (some of us knew them quite well but we didn't mind a refresher course). My expectations of a little regal grandeur were sufficiently appeased when the employee who ushered us into the box told me, in hushed tones: "Where you're sitting—General de Gaulle sat last month, and next to him, the Bavarian *Ministerpräsident*!"

More recently I had a seat in the parterre when the Prime Minister of China, Hua Kuo-feng, paid a state visit to Munich. He, too, sat in the royal box beside the *Ministerpräsident.* In other parts of Germany, I noticed, he had been shown round factories and such, but here in Munich an evening at the opera was clearly considered one of the high points of his stay. The audience had, as usual, dressed in its festive best. Looking around me I got the impression that each member of this diamond-studded assembly regarded him or herself as a sort of official greeter and, accordingly, the whole house broke into deafening applause when the Chinese delegation took their seats. Before the curtain rose the orchestra played *three* national anthems: the Chinese was unfamiliar to me and so complex that I doubt if even Mozart could have written it down at first hearing; the German anthem followed; and then came the Bavarian national anthem, *"Gott mit dir, du Land der Bayern"* (God be with thee, thou land of Bavarians).

The organizers had, moreover, cancelled the scheduled performance of *Madame Butterfly* that evening. Instead, the Chinese Prime Minister was treated to the one-act opera *Salome*, by the foremost of Munich-born composers, Richard Strauss. Perhaps a mock-Japanese Italian opera would indeed have been inappropriate to the occasion, but since this was, as I understand it, Hua's first experience with Western-style opera, I could not help wondering what he must have made of the whole thing.

It strikes me as rather ironic that Strauss's *Salome*, with its Dance of the Seven Veils, is now considered suitable fare for the honorific reception of distinguished guests: at the beginning of the century it was one of the works with which Strauss scandalized the entire operatic establishment, not least the citizens of Munich. But time is a great healer, especially among opera audiences, and if Munich just missed being the *Mozartstadt* and the Wagner centre, it has certainly made up for it by becoming the Strauss city *par excellence.* If one wants to see Strauss done to perfection, this is the place to come for everything from *Salome* to *Arabella* (after which one of the city's largest hotels is named) and *Capriccio*, which had its world première in the Opera House in 1942, and which the composer himself described as his operatic "last will and testament".

Strauss's musical life began and ended here in the Munich Opera House.

He was, as it were, to the manner born, for his father was the first horn player of the Munich court orchestra for almost 50 years, and in that capacity played a very considerable role in the Wagner productions, all of which demanded virtuoso playing from the first horn.

Richard afterwards remembered Franz Strauss as a musician of exceptional abilities. "My father was, as regards beauty and volume of tone, perfection of phrasing, and technique, one of the most notable of horn players." Strauss's mother was also musical: she was the daughter of one of the great Munich beer brewers, Georg Pschorr, whose family was famous for its interest in the arts, and it was from her that Strauss received his first piano lessons at the age of four. (The house in the Altheimer Eck, in one of the oldest parts of Munich, where Strauss was born on June 11, 1864, is no longer standing. On the ground floor there was a restaurant, the Pschorr-Bräu Bierhallen, that belonged to Strauss's grandfather.)

Strauss's youth coincided with one of the happiest eras of Munich chamber music, when both composers and players were encouraged by the interest of an affluent and educated middle class. When he was still a small boy he began taking part in the Pschorr family's weekly musicales. "As soon as he was able," a member of the family recalled, "Richard played the piano or first or second violin. Naturally Richard's compositions were also played: Tante Johanna sang the songs he dedicated to her. The high point of these family festivities, which brought together numerous relatives, was the obligatory meal of bock beer and *Würstln* following the Corpus Christi procession, in the home of Onkel Georg on the Marienplatz. For the true Münchner of that day, bock beer and sausage were as natural a conclusion to the procession as an *amen* to a prayer."

Strauss graduated from first-desk violinist in his father's amateur orchestra, the *Wilde Gung'l*, to become assistant conductor, then royal *Kapellmeister*, at the Munich Opera. For a time he specialized in symphonic music, and all his experiences had a way of turning into tone-poems: a visit to Italy engendered the fantasy *Aus Italien*, a tour of the mountains provided the inspiration for the "Alpine" Symphony, and his domestic fortunes as husband of the temperamental singer Pauline de Ahna, are described in the *Sinfonia Domestica*. Its setting is a typical Munich household of the art nouveau epoch at the turn of the century; it has a baby gurgling happily in its bath, a glockenspiel "clock" chiming the hours, and a husband-and-wife argument disguised as a double fugue.

But the theatrical heritage that Strauss had acquired as part of his Munich birthright drew him inexorably towards the writing of operas. *Salome* brought him notoriety, then fame; after *Elektra*, produced in 1909, it became apparent that "Richard the Second" was the most important German operatic composer since Wagner; his *Rosenkavalier* of 1911 was the last grand-scale opera to attract a worldwide mass audience.

In Munich, and not only at the opera, they take justifiable pride in

Born in Munich in 1895, Carl Orff (above) has become one of Germany's most prestigious and influential modern composers, famed for his treatments of the texts of medieval songs. The unusual stage sets for Orff's "Catulli Carmina" (above, right) and "Carmina Burana" (below, right) were created by Vienna State Opera designer Helmut Jürgens for the productions mounted by the Bavarian State Opera in 1959.

cultivating the music of this "last romantic" whose extraordinary career spanned so many decades of brilliant music-making. It comes as something of a shock to realize that Strauss's Opus 1 *Festmarsch* was composed in 1876, while his "Four Last Songs" are dated 1948. I remember writing his obituary in September 1949: an editor with a strongly developed sense of the dramatic headlined it "Richard Strauss: Delayed Curtain on an Era". He had been extraordinarily active almost to the very end. Earlier that year he had celebrated his 85th birthday at his country villa in Garmisch, the resort town 50 miles from Munich, had received an honorary doctorate from the University of Munich, and had conducted the Opera orchestra in excerpts from *Der Rosenkavalier* which were later included in a film made about him, appropriately entitled *A Life for Music.*

It had been, indeed, one of the most intensive and productive lives in the history of music. Somehow his works managed to sum up the energy and *Lebenslust* that have always marked the Münchner's determined pursuit of the arts—a tradition that seems to owe as much to carnival pranks and festival processions, complete with bock beer and *Würstln*, as to more formal influences such as Wagner's theories of the "total work of art".

Strauss's successor in the Munich tradition of music-making became internationally known during the early 1950s, but I suspect that it was the advent of the long-playing record rather than the theatre that first made Carl Orff a household word. I can recall when hi-fi living rooms all over Europe and America suddenly began to reverberate with the riotous sounds of a Bacchanalian revel, sung in lusty bar-room Latin and German. They were settings of the poems of medieval wandering scholar-poets who freely extolled the virtues of drink, sex and springtime. Musically, nothing quite like it had been heard before—at least, not in respectable concert halls: some of the songs in the *Carmina Burana* were sung in the dulcet tones of a love goddess awakening from sleep, others sounded as though a squad of angry men were pounding on stone with hammers and chisels.

When I first met Carl Orff in Munich 20 years ago, he told me how he had come to write this extraordinary modern setting of 13th-Century verses. The lyrics were preserved by the scribes of the Benedictine monastery of Benediktbeuern in Bavaria, south of Munich: hence the name *Carmina Burana* (Songs of Beuern). "The manuscript had been famous among literary scholars since its rediscovery in 1803," he told me. "They used to quote little pieces of it in textbooks. But it was not really alive because one important element was missing: the music. Whenever folk songs lose their music they wind up on the library shelf." His work, he felt, restored the original balance: "Music is an indispensable function of such poetry." And he made his accompaniments so percussive for a practical reason: drums and xylophones don't cover up the texts. "Horns and strings blanket the sound of words," he explained, "percussion emphasizes it."

Couples in 18th-Century costume stroll outside the floodlit entrance of Schloss Haimhausen during Munich's annual summer Rococo Ball, put on by dealers belonging to the International Salon of Antiquities. As well as being hired out for private functions, the 18th-Century castle, 16 miles north of Munich, is a delightful setting for frequent public concerts of classical music.

The *Carmina Burana* consists of a set of independent poems without any story-line, but Orff—a true Münchner, who was born here in 1895 of an old Bavarian family—conceived of his score not as a mere recital but as a dramatic production, with scenery and costumes. "These poems can't be declaimed on a concert platform," he said. "They have to be acted out. Take the drinking episode: could that be carried off in white tie and tails? You need costumes, miming, body movement. The theatre is the only place where words, music and gesture can make their full impact."

Photographs of Orff tend to stress his magisterial side—his cerebral forehead and stern, hawk-like gaze. What the camera usually fails to capture is the puckish Munich wit that makes him a genial host and brilliant conversationalist. When I first met him he brought to mind those resourceful schoolmasters one still encounters in remote Alpine villages, men who can quote Virgil or lead a climbing expedition with equal facility.

Later I came to realize that this mountaineer of the arts was primarily a poet: his texts were not subordinate to the music, as librettos have been ever since the dawn of opera. With Orff, words and music stand on an equal footing; his music is the work of a composer who loves the sheer sound of words and the magical meanings they can convey. "With everything I write it's not a question of music but of ideas," he explained. "Just to make music by itself doesn't interest me."

In a curious way, the Carl Orff phenomenon meant that music in Munich had come full circle, for his *Carmina Burana* resembled nothing so much as the colourful court pageants of the Renaissance, with all their majestic pomp, joyous excess and lavish ostentation.

Munich is still unquestionably Germany's most considerable opera centre and the State Opera is one of the world's leading opera houses,

Guest artists at the National Theatre rehearse a scene from Act Two of the dramatic opera "Iphigenia in Tauris", composed in 1779 by Bavarian-born Christoph von Gluck. In this controversial modern interpretation by the East German producer Achim Freyer, Danish soprano Lisbeth Balslev sings the role of Iphigenia; with her on stage are the German tenor Siegfried Jerusalem as Orestes (left) and the Swedish tenor Claes Ahnsjö playing Pylades.

comparable to Covent Garden in London, New York's Met and La Scala, Milan. It receives the highest subsidy of any opera house in Germany: more than 36 million marks ($9 million) a year to underwrite a budget of some 65 million marks, with which a repertoire of more than 50 operas is produced. The director of the company, the *Staatsintendant*, enjoys a positively Napoleonic status and, unlike the masters of revels who served the old kings, electors and dukes, a modern *Intendant* is not dependent on the moods and eccentricities of an unpredictable monarch—although of course he has to deal with committees and budgets. Yet, in the last analysis, his only real responsibility is towards his company and his audience.

The State Opera's long-established traditions do not prevent it from innovating and experimenting in its productions. For example, Debussy's Pelléas and Mélisande were taken out of the pseudo-Middle Ages in which they had traditionally languished since the opera's début in 1902; instead they appeared in a magical production that cast them as tragic characters from the composer's own Symbolist epoch. Similarly, Gluck's 18th-Century classic *Iphigenia in Tauris* was seized by the scruff of the neck and treated to a thorough shaking up. Early Dali and the Surrealists provided the idiom for the design: Iphigenia became a monstrously tall priestess, walking about on stilts, her face ravaged by make-up; the two heroes, Orestes and Pylades, wore something that looked like a cross between lederhosen and a parachute harness; and the evil King Thoas sported an extra pair of arms like the villains in eastern dance-drama.

I remember how exciting it was to see the dress rehearsal of *Iphigenia*. It was one of those moments of theatrical pandemonium that are not easily forgotten: the conductor in the pit, shouting *"Espressivo! Espressivo!"* to a dutiful orchestra; the director at his desk in the darkened theatre, issuing instructions to the singers and stage crew over his public-address system; the seats of the theatre filled with other members of the company, eager to find out what was going on—the dressers and make-up girls in their white smocks, the members of the *corps de ballet* and the chorus, sitting back to watch the others in moments when they were not needed on stage; the worried publicity people and the director's attachés and assistants, in various stages of exhaustion, anxiety or anticipation.

A scene is repeated two or three times; tempers flare; voices warning about the lack of time come wafting through the public-address system (there is never enough time for rehearsals in any theatre I have ever known). And during the lunch-break everyone rushes off to the underground canteen, where the singers can duly refuel on good-sized portions of *Schweinebraten* (roast pork) washed down with—needless to say—quantities of excellent Munich beer.

As I returned to the theatre for the third act, it occurred to me that an institution of this kind, which is simply taken for granted in a city like Munich, is in fact an extraordinary phenomenon: this nexus of relationships, of workers and watchers, of singers, players, dancers, painters, is to me one of the most remarkable examples of human co-operation and co-ordination to be found anywhere in this world. Yet money alone could not have brought it about: it is the product, in a very real sense, of that inexplicable thing that is called tradition, compounded of "Sorry, my boy, no vacancy", "Eternally, your Ludwig", Richard Strauss's bock beer and Orlando di Lasso's processional music.

For Carl Orff's 80th birthday in 1975, some of his friends and admirers commissioned a bust of the composer to be added to the pantheon of composers and conductors that adorn the upstairs foyer of the Opera House. When Orff was brought to see it, on the morning of his birthday, he turned to his effigy in bronze and said:

"There are certain things that simply can't be done with money. . . . There is one thing that can't be bought, not even with a great deal of money. And that is a tradition. And a tradition is something unbelievably important today, because in many things we have remained so poor."

Fooling the Eye

PHOTOGRAPHS BY ASHVIN GATHA

Painted on two solid walls of a courtyard off the Karlstrasse, a row of trompe-l'oeil houses seems to recede into the distance around a sham corner.

Munich has long been a city renowned for its well-kept appearance and its citizens take conspicuous pride in keeping it bright, clean and cheerful. But, once they had restored many war-damaged buildings, they were still faced with eyesores common to modern cities: large exposed areas of masonry, such as the backs of houses and the temporary walls fronting development sites. To solve this aesthetic problem, Münchners have turned to a tradition of *trompe-l'oeil* art dating back to the decorative conceits employed in many of their baroque public buildings and have given it a modern application: sham façades, usually commissioned by local businesses. The resulting illusions are enhanced by ingenious techniques that use perspective to create three-dimensional vistas—sometimes populated, and always amusing.

Intriguing false upper windows and a deceptive canopy, all painted on a bare wall, enhance a café entrance.

Two patient café customers wait to be served outside the fake gateway of an imaginary residence painted on a blank wall in a Karlstrasse courtyard.

Contrasting paint and incising in new plaster serve to reproduce the hewn stonework of the original 19th-Century façade for the Opera Hotel in the city

centre, which had suffered from neglect and war damage.

The grille of a vintage Mercedes appears to peek out from garage doors under a classical colonnade.

STEFAN MOSES

Fictitious residents of a magnificent building, painted in convincing detail on a Frauenstrasse wall, look down on a real-life roadsweeper.

Elegantly dressed in 18th-Century lace and mob-caps, two life-like ladies and their cats gaze from painted windows above a shop near the Marienplatz.

4

A Rich Heritage in the Arts

The district of Schwabing lies just north of central Munich. It differs little from other residential areas of the city; but intellectually, emotionally and socially it is in a class by itself, as the one clearly identifiable artists' quarter in the whole of Germany. In Europe only the Left Bank in Paris can match Schwabing's history as a gathering-place for painters, poets, writers, composers, actors and wits. Between 1890 and 1914, Schwabing's artistic legion brought to the city a fervour of activity in which all Munich's creative minds played a part—from cabaret entertainers like the Chaplinesque dialect comedian, Karl Valentin, to the most serious literati such as the novelist Thomas Mann and the poet Stefan George.

Although that time of special ferment has passed, Schwabing remains a very special place; as with Montparnasse and Greenwich Village, its reputation persists, and writers and artists who can afford the astronomical rents congregate there. It remains the focal point of the city's intellectual and artistic life, which spills over into other areas—especially Haidhausen, across the river, where life is measurably cheaper, and into Maxvorstadt, the *Vorstadt* (suburb) named after King Maximilian I, which lies between Schwabing and the city centre. Maxvorstadt contains both the University of Munich, with some 40,000 students, which was established in the capital by Ludwig I in 1826, and the Technical University, with 15,000 more. Here, too, is the largest book collection in Germany, the Bavarian State Library, with its priceless hoard of manuscripts going back to the 9th Century (among them the *Carmina Burana* that Carl Orff set to music). Beside it stands another citadel of scholarship, the State Archives, with their vast repositories of public records and of the private papers of the Wittelsbachs.

Leavening this potent mix of Bohemia and Academia are student pubs and restaurants, bookshops, avant-garde cinemas, print galleries and antique shops. Artists work next door to philosophy seminars, and long-haired poets or political science students gaze deeply into the eyes of young women law students over their glasses of beer.

Long ago Schwabing was a farming village just north of Munich's city wall. The name is said to derive from a clansman named Swapo ("The Swabian") who founded the village about A.D. 500. But its modern history begins with the construction of the so-called Suresnes Schlösschen, the "little château" commissioned in 1718 by Ignaz von Wilhelm, cabinet secretary to the Elector Max Emanuel. While the Elector and his secretary were in France as allies of Louis XIV during the War of the Spanish Succession, they spent a happy summer at the Château de Suresnes north of

The versatile talents of Karl Valentin, here seen in a typically ill-fitting outfit playing a bassoon, made him one of the legendary cabaret artistes of Munich's theatres and beer-halls in the 1920s and 1930s. A prolific writer and performer of more than 400 plays and sketches, Valentin gave comic voice to the bewilderment of the "little man" faced with the complexities of everyday life in post-First World War Germany.

Versailles and, after their return to Bavaria, von Wilhelm had his own architects build him a copy of Suresnes overlooking the swift-running stream that separated his property from what is now the English Garden. The château still stands and is used as a school today; it has seen Schwabing grow from a hamlet of some 500 souls into a modern "city within a city".

The Schwabingers have always liked to consider their community more progressive than the city that loomed to the south. Schwabing was the proud possessor of Munich's first electric tramway and of Germany's first fully automatic telephone system; as early as the mid-1890s one could actually dial one's neighbour without recourse to an operator. But before then, in 1890, when Schwabing's population had grown to 11,500, it had already become apparent that this township on the city's doorstep could not continue indefinitely to be self-sufficient, and so it was duly absorbed into Greater Munich. Thereafter, Schwabing rapidly became a Mecca for artists, for it combined the advantages of living in one of Europe's art capitals with the peace and quiet of a countrified suburb. Close by were the open fields, farmhouses and running streams of the rural world from which generations of Munich artists have drawn important inspiration.

Once the influx of painters and writers had begun, it snowballed as others followed—from northern Germany, from Scandinavia, from Russia—to profit from the stimulation of each other's presence. Within just a few years Schwabing, and Munich itself, rivalled Montmartre and Paris as bywords throughout Europe for striking originality in literature, design, art, political satire and entertainment.

How can I best introduce this patchwork of activity? With the startling abstract canvases of the painters Kandinsky and Klee? With the astringent political cartoons of the satirical weekly *Simplicissimus*? With the wit and invective of the cabaret also named *Simplicissimus*? No, it seems best to start with one of Munich's own painters, Franz Stuck, whose work conveniently embraces both the traditional and the modern. Stuck was one of the young innovators who, in the 1890s, first brought Munich into the European cultural limelight; yet he also attained the established status accorded to such "painter-princes" as Wilhelm and Friedrich von Kaulbach, and Franz von Lenbach. He built for himself in 1898 a splendid villa in Bogenhausen—across the river from the English Garden—and that villa today is the perfect place to seek a sense of the world he lived in.

A portrait of Franz von Stuck (above), who pioneered the Symbolist art movement in Germany, looks out from its "trompe-l'œil" frame of pillars and centaurs in the Villa Stuck. Built in 1898 by the artist, the house is now a museum of his work. A panel in the music room (right), in which two figures dance with Bacchic abandon to Pan's pipe music, exemplifies Stuck's distinctive blend of erotic modernism and themes from classical mythology

Sunday morning in the Villa Stuck. The sun streams in through the windows and a Brahms violin sonata floats through the room. (I have arrived during a private recital being held in one of the villa's chambers.) The mingled perfumes worn by several elegant ladies in the audience intrigue my senses, and a roomful of pictures and sculptures invites the eye.

Stuck's popularity coincided with a golden age for builders. Munich's population more than trebled—to 556,000—between 1870 and 1908.

And, of course, the construction boom paid dividends to the artists, artisans and kitsch-merchants who supplied en masse the ornamental sculptures, frescos, paintings and bric-à-brac without which any respectable new house of the time would have appeared naked and *déclassé*. The prevailing passion was for schools of earlier epochs. In parts of Munich today one sometimes feels caught in a blizzard of such styles: neo-Grecian, neo-Roman, neo-Romanesque, neo-Gothic, neo-Renaissance, neo-rococo—the architect of the Protestant Lukaskirche, in 1893, even managed to pull off the seemingly impossible trick of designing a church that was Romanesque on the outside and Gothic on the inside.

Stuck's own villa is a perfect expression both of his time and of himself. He spent years turning the place into a temple for his own florid personality, for his works, and for his beautiful and demanding wife, Mary, née Hoose, of Brooklyn, New York. The house has been described as "a personal record of the artist's graduation" from the neoclassicism of the preceding era to the art nouveau symbolism of which Stuck was one of the originators. The villa is an extraordinary *mélange* of elements and influences—Greek, Roman, Egyptian and Byzantine, all happily crowded side by side. The portico is supported by Doric columns, the garden is filled with copies of Greek busts surmounting stone pillars and the entrance hall is ornamented with Greek bas-reliefs.

"Please do not touch the sculptures," the attendant reminds us. But we have already discovered that they are made not of marble but of plaster. Stuck took copies of Greek gods and maenads, nymphs and satyrs and coloured them to suit himself, as though they were his own sculptures. However, he also composed his own friezes of centaurs and Amazons that are strangely dualistic creatures of the *fin de siècle*: healthy Munich lads and sensuous Munich lasses transposed into the Aeolian mode.

The villa's Music Room suggests a setting for a Hellenic fertility cult. Hardly a square inch of wall space has been left undecorated. The surfaces are divided into an intricate pattern of panels, on which Stuck painted dancers and musicians, male and female, conveying the playful sensuality that made him such a popular figure on the Munich art scene. There are, for example, two naiads on a seesaw: one of them has dispensed with her clothes altogether, while the other is concentrating more on energetic see-sawing than on keeping her gown up. Nearby, Orpheus charms wild beasts—including crocodiles—with his playing. The names of Mozart, Beethoven, Handel, Wagner et al. are emblazoned on the walls in golden letters.

Stuck's notoriety as a painter came early in his career. A fresh wind of artistic innovation had been blowing from the west—from Paris and Brussels, where artists like Monet, Rodin and Redon were producing an original and demanding kind of work: symbolic, self-assertive, "decadent". In 1892, responding to the new breeze, a group of young Munich painters, with the 29-year-old Stuck as a prime mover, seceded from Munich's

In this 1897 illustration for the satirical Munich weekly "Simplicissimus", a queue of women (on the left), dressed according to the conventions of the time, step into the Fountain of Youth and emerge (on the right) costumed as they would be presented in the pages of the avant-garde magazine "Jugend" (Youth). The artist, Bruno Paul, was commenting on the great influence the periodical had on design, giving its name to the German art nouveau movement—Jugendstil.

powerful exhibition group of established artists, headed by the elderly and immensely influential Lenbach, and founded a rival association known as the *Secession*—a name afterwards adopted by similar breakaway groups in Vienna, Dresden and Berlin.

Just around the corner from the villa's Music Room hangs the most famous of all Stuck's paintings (or one version of it; he did several). Entitled *Sin*, it portrays a sultry nude with a large black snake draped around her shoulders—a real boa instead of a feather one. This *femme fatale* in her sumptuous gilded frame looks one straight in the eye, no matter where one stands in the room, and the summons is as unmistakable as a First World War recruiting poster. The picture was painted while the artist was still establishing his reputation and, when it was first exhibited in 1893, it caused a flutter, for its frank yet sinister allure was calculated to flout the decorum of the preceding age. Stuck was soon after established as a leader of the German branch of the international movement of Symbolist artists, who dealt in the images of their dream world.

It says a good deal for the open-mindedness of the Bavarian Prince-Regent, Luitpold, that, despite the agitation over *Sin*, within a year of its exhibition he did not hesitate to commission Stuck to paint his portrait—a form of official recognition that was to prove an important step in Stuck's elevation to "painter-prince".

In spite of his avant-garde stance, Stuck never did stray too far from the mainstream of Munich painting or the taste of the public, just as he always retained a clear allegiance to the progress of his own career. He became the most fashionable—and expensive—portrait painter of his day. When he was only 32 years of age he was appointed a professor at the Munich Academy of Fine Arts. He became immensely rich, gave huge dinner parties to which members of the Bavarian cabinet were often invited, and in 1905 he was ennobled, becoming Franz von Stuck.

There is a painting in the Villa Stuck that records what must have been one of the proudest moments of the artist's life: the torchlight procession organized by his students and well-wishers on his 50th birthday, February 23, 1913. Stuck painted the scene as though he were standing across the road, watching the massed torches of the crowd cast their dull glow against the darkened façade of his house; he himself is portrayed in splendid isolation on the balcony, a dark figure silhouetted against the light of his studio on the first floor.

Few other painters have ever received such spectacular and spontaneous acclaim so early in their careers. Just over a year later he added a second imposing wing to his princely residence, but virtually at the moment of its completion the First World War broke out, and in its wake came Germany's defeat and revolution.

Stuck narrowly escaped being shot as a hostage during the uncertain days of political struggle immediately after the war and, during the decade before his death in 1928, he witnessed the waning of his popularity and the collapse of the whole aesthetic on which his career had been predicated. At his funeral they spoke of him, quite rightly, as "the last of the painter-princes of the great days of Munich".

An ink-and-watercolour sketch of a rider on horseback, by the Russian-born painter Wassily Kandinsky, provided an appropriate cover motif for the 1912 almanac of Der Blaue Reiter (the Blue Rider) group of artists. Published in Munich, the almanac was edited by Kandinsky and Münchner Franz Marc. It contained lavishly illustrated essays that advanced the latest ideas on painting, music and theatre and reflected the vibrant new mood permeating the arts prior to the outbreak of the First World War in 1914.

But, during Stuck's heyday in the 1890s, Munich's artistic revolution had really taken fire. The energy of his originality was rapidly absorbed and extended by other artists and by a host of intellectuals and dissidents (among them, briefly, Lenin and Trotsky) who flooded in from Russia, Hungary, the Baltic and the Balkans, eager to escape the increasingly oppressive conditions of their homelands. Many of these newcomers, collectively referred to by the Münchners as Schlawiner (Slavs), took up residence in Schwabing. And, in 1896, two publications—*Jugend* and *Simplicissimus*—first appeared; together they provided the forum that Munich's artists, designers, writers and satirists needed.

Of the two publications, *Jugend* appeared first, on January 1, 1896. Its very title, "Youth", amounted to an affront to the older generation. Many of the contributors to this paean to the new art were not painters but graphic designers, who found inspiration not in the "great tradition" championed by Lenbach but in Japanese styles, in French and English art nouveau, and in commercial art. This heady mixture produced pictures that sometimes bore only a superficial resemblance to their subject matter, and threatened to disappear altogether amid a welter of ornamental devices, stylized wave-forms and clinging tendrils. From that point on, any art nouveau work—painted or printed, whether from Munich or the outside world—came to be known in Germany as *Jugendstil*, a word meaning literally "in the style of *Jugend* illustrations".

Jugend also startled its contemporaries with a new ingredient: overt sexuality. Week after week, in the most brilliant and subtle colour lithography, it published the sumptuous nudes of Stuck and his fellow Symbolist artists—forest nymphs, mermaids, "allegories of the dance"—drawn with a full-frontal boldness and sensuousness of line that gave the *Jugendstil* nude a particular cachet. All this was far too explicit for traditionalists such as the aging Lenbach, who was heard to complain that everything was being instantly undressed and revealed; people no longer understood "the fascination of the half-concealed".

It seemed at the time that nothing could possibly trump the audacities of the *Jugendstil* avant-garde. And yet, further innovation was already in the making. Since 1893, a group of painters who had settled in the little country village of Dachau, eight miles north-west of Munich, had been experimenting with forms suggested by the landscape surrounding them. Some of their mature works—notably those of Adolf Hölzel—utilizing slender vertical tree trunks rising from the thin rolling mists of the moors, approached a pure formality of design that showed a turning towards abstraction. But it was with the work of two of Stuck's own pupils, the Russian Wassily Kandinsky and the Swiss Paul Klee, that abstract art made its first real appearance in Munich.

Even now, three generations after the fact, I am still surprised and dazzled by the intensity of the upheaval that shook art in Munich at the beginning of the 20th Century. Nowhere is the whole exciting process better illustrated than at the Städtische Galerie in the Lenbachhaus, that spacious villa in which one can stroll past the last two centuries of Munich's art in more or less chronological order: the landscape paintings and the history paintings, the court portraits and the Symbolist allegories, followed by the *Jugendstil* pictures with their erotic overtones.

But then one opens the next door and is met by an explosion of primary colours that leaves one fairly gasping for breath. These are Kandinsky's pictures: the visual equivalent of a cold shower after a warm bath. It was Kandinsky who led the way into a world of bright colours and abstract designs reminiscent of the Russian peasant toys of his youth. Born in Moscow in 1866, Kandinsky came to Munich at the age of 30. After more than a decade spent studying and experimenting in Munich and elsewhere in Europe, he was joined by a young Munich painter, Franz Marc, with whom, in 1911, he launched an exhibition entitled *Der Blaue Reiter* (The Blue Rider), showing works of like-minded artists. The name was also to be the title of their almanac, an anthology of essays and illustrations published jointly by Kandinsky and Marc six months later—a work now regarded as one of the most important art manifestos of the century.

Who, or what, was the original Blue Rider? A guard at the Lenbachhaus once told me, rather irritably, that people were forever asking him where the Blue Rider was, since there is a sign bearing that legend with an arrow pointing to one of the exhibition rooms, indicating "This Way to the Blue Rider"; and yet there was nothing of the sort to be seen in any of the works on display. Theories abound to account for the choice of name. Kandinsky's own explanation is simple: he invented the name with Franz Marc while sitting around a coffee table in Marc's house: "We both loved blue, Marc liked horses and I riders. So the name came by itself. And after that, Frau Maria Marc's fabulous coffee tasted even better." In due course, the name came to be applied to the whole group of painters associated with Kandinsky and Marc, among them Paul Klee, Marianne von Werefkin, Alexei von Jawlensky, August Macke and Gabriele Münter.

When Kandinsky began to paint the cover illustration for their almanac, he dashed off a design for a coloured woodcut close in its charm and naïvety to the Russian folk prints that played such an important role in his own evolution as an artist. The book's contents, however, were much more deliberate and ambitious. Franz Marc wrote in one of his contributions to the book that "art concerns itself with the most profound matters, and its renewal cannot be merely one of form but the rebirth of thought itself. *Mysticism* has been awakened in our souls and with it the most primal elements of art." They had, he said, discovered the path to a "new art".

At first, some critics and most of the public were unreceptive to the Blue Rider canvases, to the bright reds that clashed with untrammelled greens and yellows, to the vivid landscapes of Kandinsky and Gabriele Münter (the woman who was Kandinsky's intimate friend for many years), to Klee's mysterious interiors, to Marc's red and blue horses, to the dreamlike street scenes of August Macke. But a number of people in the world of modern art, including dealers and patrons, realized at once that in these astonishing works something quite extraordinary was afoot. Two years after the almanac was first published, Marc was able to write in his introduction to the second edition that the Blue Riders had been vindicated. With an optimism that now seems hopelessly idealistic, he asserted that the path taken by the group, in spite of ridicule and incomprehension, was "the main avenue of human development"; they were constantly striving for "an inward stillness in the turbulence of their time".

The date of Marc's progress report was March 1914. Soon there was no stillness to be found anywhere in Europe. The First World War made short work of this gentle and brilliant community of spirits. Almost immediately Macke was killed on the Western Front. Franz Marc was a casualty during the terrible bloodletting at Verdun in 1916. Klee survived because he was lucky enough to be assigned to a support unit behind the lines. One of the

Two visitors to Munich's municipal art gallery in the Lenbachhaus respond in their own ways to a roomful of Kandinsky paintings that form part of a comprehensive collection of works by the seminal Blaue Reiter group. The Kandinskys in the gallery constitute the single largest assemblage in Germany of the artist's output, most of them donated in 1957 by the foremost woman member of the Blaue Reiter circle, Kandinsky's close companion Gabriele Münter.

minor Russian Blue Riders, Vladimir Burliuk, was killed during the fighting in the Balkans. The Russians Jawlensky and Werefkin were forced into exile in neutral Switzerland. Kandinsky returned to Russia, where he later joined in the artistic movements of the early Soviet State; he came back to Germany after the war, again in 1933 but left with the rise of Hitler.

The fate of the Blue Riders reflected the fate of Europe as a whole. Although much interesting work was done in Munich during the 1920s, the city never again saw an artistic flowering to match the heady years before the First World War; the dictatorship imposed by the Nazis, with their infamous decrees against "degenerate art", saw to that. It is only over the last three decades that Munich has once again emerged as a capital that nourishes art and artists.

The very same year that saw the birth of *Jugend* also saw the birth of the satirical weekly *Simplicissimus*, which in time was to usurp the former's place as Germany's leading avant-garde medium, as *Jugend* itself gradually became relatively sedate and predictable. *Simplicissimus* was graphically one of the most exciting magazines ever published in any country; it carried works by the leading designers, artists and writers of the period, both native Münchners and those who had been attracted from further afield by Munich's liveliness. One of the best-known editors, Ludwig Thoma, was a Bavarian playwright who won a nationwide reputation for his dialect stories and plays; its regular contributors included the novelists Heinrich and Thomas Mann and Henrik Ibsen.

Simpl, as its readers called it, initially cost a mere 10 pfennigs but every issue was the event of the week. Middle-class Munich and, before long, all middle-class Germany, were divided between those who couldn't stand having the sheet in the house and those who couldn't live without it. Periodically there would be a national uproar over a *Simpl* cartoon or satire that tweaked the upturned moustaches of the Hohenzollern Kaiser in Berlin. In 1898, the editors were hauled into court for ridiculing the Kaiser on his taste for wearing exotic costumes on a trip to Jerusalem. The publisher Albert Langen, who later lived in Schwabing's Mandlstrasse, fled to Paris. Thomas Theodor Heine, who drew the offending cover, and Frank Wedekind, who wrote the accompanying verses, were both sentenced to six months' imprisonment for *lèse-majesté*. (Wedekind, one of the many prominent writers to be associated with *Simpl* in its prime, was a playwright of great inventive power who combined satirical attacks on the morals of Munich's bourgeois society with a new freedom of erotic expression.)

But of all the writers who owed a debt to *Simpl*, the most celebrated was Thomas Mann. His mother came to Munich in 1893. The widow of a successful businessman from Lübeck, she had to rely for a livelihood on the interest earned by her husband's estate. In Munich she found the cost of living low enough for her to keep her five children in an eight-room apartment attended by a small staff of servants. She settled in Rambergstrasse almost, though not quite, in Schwabing, close to Ludwig I's Siegestor—the Victory Gate that marks the boundary between Schwabing and old Munich. Her oldest son, Heinrich, was already fending for himself as a budding writer. Thomas, then 18, spent some months as a clerk in an insurance office before he, too, managed to persuade his mother to let him try his hand at being a freelance writer. The Munich of that epoch provided the ideal environment for a struggling writer, if only because avant-garde magazines were eager to print stories and poems by unknown talents.

To young Thomas, Munich seemed a wholly enchanting city. "Munich shone," begins a short story he wrote in 1902. "A sky of blue satin stretched radiantly over a city of festive squares and white-columned temples." He goes on to describe "bird songs and secret joy in all the narrow streets. . . . Many windows were open, and the sound of music issued forth from many of them. One heard people practising the piano, the violin or the cello. . . . Young people strolled in and out of the university and State Library with literary magazines in the pockets of their jackets. Art was in full flower, art was in the ascendant, art stretched its rosy sceptre over the city and smiled."

Early on in his career, Mann made himself useful as a bright young editor for *Simplicissimus*. In 1898, when the magazine's publisher, Albert Langen, had to leave Munich for Paris to escape arrest in the *lèse-majesté* case, all his editors moved up a notch and, suddenly, there was room for another assistant at a hundred marks a month. Mann was offered the position, which he held for a year. "This insolent and truly artistic sphere", as he

In this impertinent cover for the magazine "Simplicissimus", cartoonist Thomas Theodor Heine, chained and unrepentant, continues to draw for the weekly publication after being sentenced in 1898 to six months in prison for lèse-majesté. An earlier, controversial issue of the magazine had lampooned, in picture and verse, a diplomatic visit by Kaiser Wilhelm II to Palestine. Prosecution ensued against all those involved in this disparagement of royalty.

3. Jahrgang **Preis 10 Pfg.** Nummer 34

SIMPLICISSIMUS

Abonnement vierteljährlich 1 Mk. 25 Pfg. Illustrierte Wochenschrift Post-Zeitungskatalog: 5. Nachtrag Nr. 6496a.

Wie ich meine nächste Zeichnung machen werde*)

(Zeichnung von Th. Th. Heine)

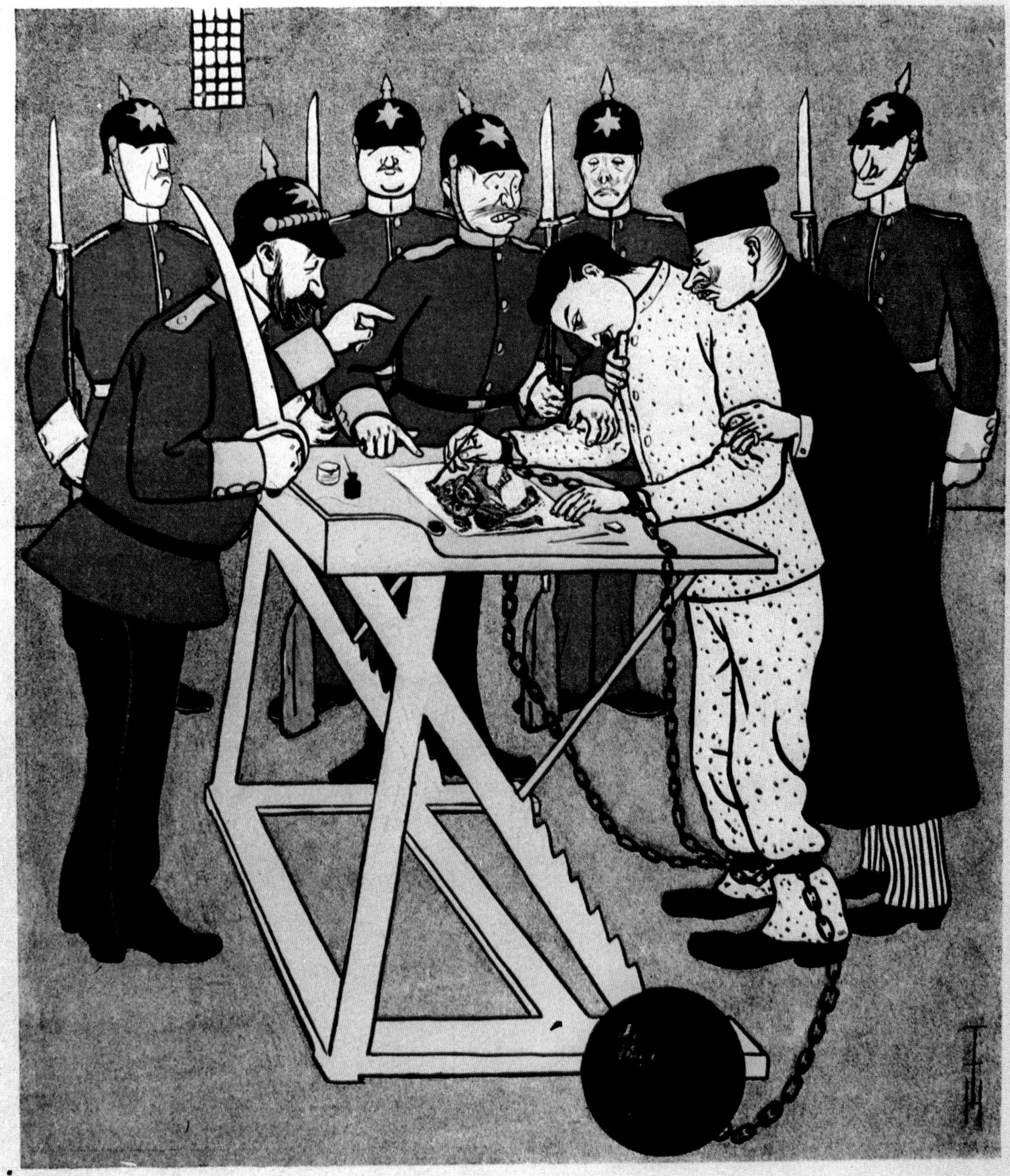

„Ernst ist das Leben, heiter die Kunst."

*) Herr Th. Th. Heine wurde am 2. November wegen angeblicher Majestätsbeleidigung in Untersuchungshaft genommen, wo er noch schmachtet.

called the world of *Simplicissimus*, made a tremendous impression on his youthful sensibilities. "My relationship to you was profound, it was almost mystical in nature," he once wrote in an open love letter to *Simplicissimus*. "I loved you before I ever saw you."

At the same time, Mann was working on *Buddenbrooks*, his first and most definitive novel, set partly in Munich. (It was singled out for mention in his Nobel Prize citation of 1929.) He moved to the very heart of Schwabing, first to the Marktstrasse, then to the Feilitzschstrasse, where he had a tiny apartment, complete with a piano (on which visiting friends could accompany him as he played the violin), and with a small portrait of Leo Tolstoy standing on his desk.

Thomas Mann was destined to preside over German literature as the great, ironic figure who represented his country's genius in the panorama of 20th-Century civilization. Understandably, once the weight of that responsibility fell on his shoulders, he ceased to fit into the casual and rather bizarre atmosphere of Schwabing. In 1905 he married the pretty and vivacious Katia Pringsheim, daughter of a well-to-do mathematics professor at the University of Munich; and although they began their married life in Schwabing (Franz-Joseph-Strasse 2), the arrival of the first four of their six children eventually led them to build a large house across the river in Bogenhausen, in what is now known as the Thomas-Mann-Allee.

In the 1890s, however, Thomas Mann's career as a writer was just beginning and the centre of the Schwabing stage was claimed by a more flamboyant figure in the German literary pantheon: the poet Stefan George, with his circle of self-important disciples. Independently wealthy, George came from Bingen, on the Rhine, and travelled a great deal, often visiting Munich. His coterie consisted of young poets who took their cue from poets of the English Pre-Raphaelite and the French Symbolist schools, especially Stéphane Mallarmé, who had befriended George in Paris. The George clique thought of their master not just as a poet but as a "priest of the spirit", a Messiah of a new religion of art. One early admirer, the poet Hugo von Hofmannsthal (Richard Strauss's librettist), praised him fulsomely for "the innate kingliness of his self-possessed soul".

George's strong right hand was the scholar-poet Karl Wolfskehl, the "Zeus of Schwabing" and an authority on ancient Greek as well as early German mythology, who kept open house in Schwabing's Römerstrasse. George would receive the homage of his followers in a room that Wolfskehl set aside for his use: the so-called *Kugelzimmer* (sphere room), which was illuminated by a single spherical lamp. George would write his poems upstairs and send them downstairs for Wolfskehl to read; Wolfskehl, in turn, would bring George his own verses.

Nowadays neither George nor Wolfskehl are taken half so seriously as they took themselves. In 1902, George fell passionately in love with a beautiful and talented 14-year-old boy, Maximilian Kronberger. "Maximin",

The distinguished novelist Thomas Mann reads at his desk in his house in Poschingerstrasse—the street has been renamed Thomas-Mann-Allee—in the Munich district of Bogenhausen. The photograph was taken about 1922. Mann had arrived from the North German seaport of Lübeck in 1893, at the age of 18, and lived in the city for the next 40 years. After a short period as an editor for "Simplicissimus" while still in his twenties, Mann established himself very quickly as an important writer with his early masterpiece "Buddenbrooks". He was awarded the Nobel Prize for Literature in 1929.

as George called him, died the following year. George thereupon glorified the boy in several volumes of poetry that are now widely dismissed as over-inflated. Wolfskehl, meanwhile, formed a new circle of writers who termed themselves the *Kosmiker*, because they liked to believe that they rarely thought of anything on a less than cosmic level.

The esoteric pretentiousness of these writers and their followers struck many onlookers as nonsensical. Perhaps they themselves would never have become aware of the true effect they had on outsiders had it not been for the irrepressible Franziska zu Reventlow, a young and independent-minded North German countess remarkable for her astringent opinions and free-spirited vitality. She arrived in Munich from Hamburg at the age of 24 with ambitions to paint; instead she wrote novels and threw herself into a heady round of affairs with intellectuals, artists and writers. She bore a child, but never revealed who the father was. To earn money—she was always broke since she had repudiated her family background—she did translations (for *Simpl*) and wrote, among other things, a series of hilarious unsigned parodies of the *Kosmiker*. Working through the night, she would personally type and duplicate her satirical sallies—they took the form of a news-sheet, the *Schwabinger Beobachter* (Schwabing Observer)—and then deposit them next morning in the mailboxes of her targets. Understandably the recipients were very upset when they finally discovered that their satirist was their much-beloved countess.

As an ironic footnote to that glorious time, it should be recalled that this same Franziska zu Reventlow, then a small star in that galaxy of luminaries, is now the most widely and avidly read woman writer of the whole period, admired especially by feminists. Her diaries and letters have become famous. She left a marvellously unvarnished account of what it was like to be a struggling writer in Schwabing; poor, ill (she had tuberculosis, which killed her in 1918 at the age of 47), an unmarried mother and a partner in a series of intense love affairs conducted in the eye of Munich's creative hurricane. In retrospect, she emerges as the most fascinating and original of her circle—beautiful and strong-willed, honest and self-doubting. As the red-haired poet Erich Mühsam—another of *Simpl's* left-wing contributors—testified, she was "a human being who knew what freedom means, a being without prejudice, without traditional inhibitions. And she was a happy being. . . . When she laughed, her mouth laughed, and her whole face, so that it was a pleasure to watch her. But her eyes, those large, deep blue eyes, remained serious and unmoved."

In her own splendid fashion, Franziska zu Reventlow summed up the qualities that made Schwabing essential to Munich, and Munich important to the rest of the world. The individualists who came here were looking not just for a comfortable place to live but for a special kind of freedom. They succeeded, for themselves and others; the majority of the ordinary citizens of Munich became so used to living with these unconventional types that they ceased to regard them as peculiar and undesirable. It was thanks to them, Mühsam said, "that all Munich grew accustomed to the eccentric, learnt tolerance and accorded the nonconformist his right to exist".

Originality appeared in many other forms besides art and literature. The most striking expression of it was in one of Schwabing's greatest traditions: cabaret. This particular form of entertainment-cum-self-expression was transplanted to Schwabing's fertile soil from its birthplace in the bars and cafés of Paris. Cabaret in Munich began in 1901 with the installation of a group calling itself *Die Elf Scharfrichter* (the Eleven Executioners) in the Golden Stag *Gasthaus* in the Türkenstrasse, a venue that was soon referred to by the name of the cabaret team. Their star performer was a *chanteuse* in the French style, Marya Delvard, who always wore a sweeping black dress with a high neck.

The whole of intellectual Munich—a minority, it should be remembered, who enjoyed flouting the standards of more conservative citizens—came to see this troupe of "wild art-gipsies", as Heinrich Mann described them: "From their cafés they brought to the stage of their Munich cabaret an attitude of supreme disdain for bourgeois man, convinced that by stealth one could inject a little literature into his life only by means of bluff, satire, devilry and at least the appearance of eroticism."

Frank Wedekind was one of those who performed at the Eleven Executioners. His act was noted for its simplicity: he accompanied himself on a lute or guitar in the casual folk-song style that has since become ubiquitous.

But "In those days," as Heinrich Mann recalled, "he was an almost terrifyingly original phenomenon"—terrifying because he was outrageously nonchalant about the pleasures and problems of this sinful life. Wedekind's work had a considerable influence on Bertolt Brecht, who was a medical student in Munich until 1917, where he wrote quantities of poetry and several of his early plays.

There was, naturally, room for more than one great cabaret in Schwabing. In 1903, Kathi Kobus, a strong-minded publican who had worked in a restaurant just down the street from the Eleven Executioners, opened her famous *Simplicissimus* cabaret, also in the Türkenstrasse; she took the name from the magazine with the blessing of its publishers and editors.

The original *Simplicissimus* cabaret was one of those cultural monuments that lives on in song and story more than in stone and mortar. The place was never much to look at—just a sort of *Gasthaus*, with an ordinary outer room and a corridor connecting it to the cabaret room at the rear, where there was a small stage, a piano and a bar, presided over by the formidable Kobus. What it lacked in architectural merit it soon made up in atmosphere. The rooms were crowded every night, "the air filled with smoke and the smell of close-packed humanity", as Mühsam remembered. "We all felt very comfortable and at home there." Kathi Kobus, who revelled in the company of the town's often impoverished artists and liked seeing their work, covered the walls with pictures she accepted in lieu of payment: serious works as well as cartoons. Thomas Theodor Heine, who had created a ferocious bulldog as the logo of the magazine, personally painted Kobus' street-sign, using the same symbol.

Originally, performances at the *Simpl* cabaret were completely improvised, and anyone with talent could perform. A bottle of *Sekt* (German champagne) would make the rounds and people would begin to recite their own poems or sing their latest cabaret songs. Erich Mühsam, for example, might recite one of his love songs in praise of girls with bow legs and frizzy hair, or offer a rhyming calendar designed for the unemployed, or one of his famous political verses. His *Der Revoluzzer*, a biting comment on the gap between political talk and political action, became one of the best-known songs of the following two decades. It concerns a lighter of street-lamps who plays at radical politics because it's the thing to do—a theoretical left-winger, in modern terms—with no understanding of what change will mean. When the revolution for which he has shouted actually materializes, he is appalled:

Aber unser Revoluzzer
Schrie: "Ich bin der Lampenputzer!
Dieses guten Leuchtelichts
Bitte, bitte, tut ihm nichts!
Wenn wir ihm das Licht ausdrehen,
Kann kein Bürger nichts mehr sehen."

This translates best as a quatrain:

Our radical he cries and stamps:
"I'm the lighter of the lamps!
Don't you touch them! Leave them be!
If you destroy them, we can't see!"

Distraught, the self-styled radical locks himself into his house to write a book on how it is possible to have a revolution *and* keep the status quo.

Another of the habitual *Simpl* poets, Ludwig Scharf—who was briefly engaged to Kathi Kobus—usually struck a belligerent revolutionary attitude when he mounted the podium, a circumstance that later did not prevent him from marrying a Hungarian countess. She too became a welcome guest at the *Simpl*; Kathi, apparently, bore no grudges. Her favourite poet, in any case, was not her former fiancé but her remarkable *Hausdichter* (house poet) Joachim Ringelnatz, who went on to become one of the foremost satirical philosopher-poets of modern Germany. Ringelnatz—who had, in his time, worked as sailor, newspaper-boy and window-cleaner—was instantly recognized by the habitués as jester-in-residence, and returned the compliment by praising Kathi Kobus and her illustrious establishment in a song that concluded:

Scheid ich einst von diesem Globus,
Sei mein letzter Abschiedsgruss:
"Pfüat di Gott, mein' Kathi Kobus!
Heil dir, Simplicissimus!"

Which means:

When I depart this earthly plane,
I'll find no reason to complain;
I'll shout: "God save you, Kathi Kobus!
Fare well, Simplicissimus!"

Perhaps inevitably, the old *Simpl* ultimately became a victim of its own popularity. Too many tourists and "slummers" heard of the place and made life difficult for the local Bohemians. Kathi Kobus did her best to keep order; described as "statuesque", she was her own bouncer and, if there were trouble-makers in the audience, she would seize them by the collar and propel them unceremoniously out of the door. Once, one of the Kaiser's sons descended on her, incognito, accompanied by a group of friends in students' uniforms. Kathi recognized them, of course, and, when they began raising a rumpus, she shocked the royal party into instant silence with a stentorian: *"Saupreiss'n, stad san!"*—"Shut up, you damn Prussians!" (To the arch-Bavarian, a Prussian is generically a *Saupreiss*—a Prussian pig—just as in Georgia and Alabama a Yankee is by definition a Damnyankee.)

Later, in an effort to return to a more pristine Bohemia, unsullied by the new commercialism, she opened *Kathis Ruh* (Kathi's Rest) on a hilltop in the bucolic precincts of suburban Wolfratshausen, 17 miles south of

In a corner of old Schwabing, traditionally the artists' quarter of Munich, three young Münchners relax beside a health-food shop whose outdoor trinket stall and notice-board provide additional attractions for their community. In spite of today's high rents and commercialization, Schwabing's Bohemian reputation still attracts writers and artists.

Munich, leaving her Schwabing cabaret to carry on under new management. Needless to say, it was never the same.

But there were other talents, other cabaret artists, notably the zany young comedian who called himself Karl Valentin (real name, Valentin Ludwig Fey) whose career was to span 40 years. Valentin had his first success in 1907 at the Restaurant Baderwirt in Dachauerstrasse. He had been apprenticed to a carpenter, an experience that evidently equipped him somehow with enough performing skill and insight to make him the comic folk genius of Munich—Germany's equivalent to Charlie Chaplin.

Like Chaplin, Valentin always played the little man caught in a world several sizes too large for him. Together with his gifted partner Liesl Karlstadt, he gave countless cabaret, vaudeville and theatre performances. Soon they were making silent films. Later, between the world wars, he and Liesl appeared in sound films, on records and on the radio. They had a knack for every type of theatrical entertainment: situation comedy, songs that echoed the Bavarian comic folk theatre, knockabout slapstick, satires on advertising slogans and parodies of government officialese, intermingled with bits of surrealism, absurdity and black humour.

But Valentin's small, gnarled voice was no match for Dr. Goebbels' humourless propaganda machine. Valentin withdrew from the public stage and did not come out of his retirement until the postwar years when, in his mid-sixties, he and Liesl Karlstadt made a brief comeback at a new *Simpl* cabaret. Valentin died in February 1948, three weeks after concluding his last run of great appearances. In Munich today there is a Valentin Museum in the Isartor—one of the city's restored medieval gate-towers—and two fountains in the Viktualienmarkt, one in honour of him and the other of Liesl Karlstadt. But the most cogent proof that Munich has not forgotten him is the fact that, on an evening when one of his films is resurrected on television, just about everyone stays at home to watch it.

Schwabing was described by Countess Reventlow as "certainly a municipal district, but only by accident". Kandinsky said, "It's a state of mind"—and that state of mind remains alive and well, permeating the whole city.

Munich is, for instance, once again a city of art. After 1945, the museums were able to acquire and exhibit brilliant works by Klee and Kandinsky, Marc and Macke, that had been prohibited during the Third Reich. Painters and sculptors were again free to express what Marc, in the first edition of the *Blue Rider*, had called "the artist's inner yearning". How far the Munich artists of recent years have profited by that freedom can be seen in the literally dozens of private and public galleries that make Munich, considering its size, one of the most art-conscious cities in the world today. Since 1945, a steady stream of new art has poured from the studios of Munich. Once again the city is a haven for many foreign artists, who work alongside the native Münchners. Perhaps the "Blue Riders" of the next wave are

Decorative Flourishes

The flowing ornamental designs espoused by the Jugendstil movement—named after the Munich periodical "Jugend" that championed the linear style—had widespread influence, but particularly on the Bavarian capital. Local designers employed plaster and paint to lavish a wealth of decorative motifs on the façades of Munich's apartment blocks and private homes.

Shown on these pages is a selection of such work, dating from 1898 to 1911 and featuring realistic and stylized figures, as well as animals and plants, that often cleverly complement the architectural features. Some examples: a huntress blows on a serpentine horn near a cauldron that billows plasterwork smoke (top row, left); colourful peacocks adorn the top of an upper window (top row, second from right); a stucco fox trots amiably over a doorway (middle row, second from right); and acanthus-leaf hair frames a monstrous face whose mouth is an oval window (bottom row, centre). The elegance of Jugendstil is captured especially well in the delicate tendrils that encircle an inverted heart-shaped window (middle row, right).

During an auction held at the Gallery Wolfgang Ketterer, an assistant holds up a 1910 woodcut by the German Expressionist Ernst Ludwig Kirchner, while the auctioneer calls for bids. The prestigious gallery, housed permanently in a wing of the Villa Stuck, organizes public sales such as this one four times a year.

already hard at work among the hundreds of known and unknown artists who now make their home in the city. There has certainly been no lack of new ideas here, and the galleries actually offer a richer and more varied harvest than at any previous time in the city's history.

Otto Wesendonck, a young sculptor who is a good friend of mine, is in no doubt about Munich's continuing artistic importance. "Of course, we have problems here," he told me, "but at least this city is alive to the possibilities of art. The atmosphere is favourable to creative people because there is a large and intelligent public that cares about the fine arts. You find them crowding every really interesting exhibition and on the whole they are very receptive to new ideas. And the government has not been remiss in sponsoring competitions that make it possible for many of us to live reasonably comfortable lives." Perhaps it has also helped the living artists of Munich that the city's curators and collectors have learnt an important lesson: those Klees and Kandinskys they could have bought in the Twenties for a handful of marks are now worth hundreds of thousands.

And Schwabing? Modern Schwabing still prides itself on its cabarets, though the style and the prices have changed: most of them are indistinguishable from the nightclubs and discothèques of other 20th-Century capitals. I heard one old man, who obviously remembered the old days, gazing with a jaundiced eye at the numerous dens now encircling the square named after Wedekind, declare that Schwabing now means *"Neon, Nylon und Nepp!"* (A *Nepplokal* is a clip-joint.)

Yet, if you know how to look for them, the qualities that originally made

Schwabing are still there; but they are more in the citizens than in the cafés and cabarets, the student dives and art studios. Of the extraordinary people I myself have met in Munich in the course of the last 30 years, a remarkable number have been Schwabingers—a baron who sells antiques, a black American actor who has devoted his life to teaching the left-behind children of black G.I.s, a beautiful folk singer with a deep, warm voice who would sing Brecht and Weill as well as the blues, a film star who had two wives and two sets of children all living in the same house with him, a mathematician who wrote detective novels in his spare time, an Englishwoman who had spent the war here looking after both her invalid German husband and Allied prisoners in a P.O.W. camp.

To be sure, there are few now of the golden generation who remain, and hardly anyone who can remember what it was like to live in the Schwabing of George, Klee, Kobus and Reventlow. Yet the special atmosphere may still, on occasion, be conjured up. Not long ago, I was invited to a garden party in Schwabing given by a film director. It was a *jour fixe*—that is a certain day of the month at which all one's friends are regularly invited to an open house, whether or not they actually bring the bottle of wine that is the normal ticket of admission. Since it was too cold to stay outdoors in the garden, we gathered inside the host's garden-house. In the rustic days of Schwabing it must have been a shed, but it was now supplied with central heating, proper furniture and oriental masks on the walls. As in days of yore, the house was packed with "Schwabylonians", as they were known (Schwabing plus Babylonians being a suitably decadent-sounding combination): editors, museum curators, writers, artists, a few fallen women and others of considerable standing, a famous actor, a newspaper cartoonist and a couple of journalists, a dealer in primitive art, a patent attorney and his wife of two weeks, a woman psychiatrist . . .

There was hardly room to drop a pin, and yet there seemed to be an abundance of mental space. Suddenly I felt a moving appreciation of the cheerful continuity of this special place in Munich and of "the beauty of the grandiose village under the melting blue of the Alpine sky", as Thomas Mann speaks of it in *Dr. Faustus*, "the suggestion it had of all-the-year-round carnival freedom". It is this sense of the grandiose village that keeps creative people coming to Munich and this year-round carnival freedom that keeps them happy.

Guest Workers Who Came to Stay

Turkish street-cleaners return in a squad at midday to the depot in central Munich after labouring since before dawn to sweep their assigned sectors of the city.

From the 1950s onwards, rapid expansion of West German industry led to severe labour shortages in manufacturing centres such as Munich. The problem was alleviated by the recruitment of *Gastarbeiter* (literally "guest workers"), from Turkey, Greece, Yugoslavia and other countries, to help man the city's factories and public services. Although the slowing down of the German "economic miracle" in the 1970s led to a ban on further recruitment, the hard-working *Gastarbeiter* and their dependants accounted for 10 per cent of Munich's population in 1980. Cut off from their German neighbours by barriers of language and custom, the newcomers have crowded into the poorer areas of town, creating immigrant quarters complete with clubs, places of worship and ethnic food shops, where they can pursue familiar patterns of life.

A Turk, one of the many immigrants employed in Munich as dustmen, returns two bins he has just emptied.

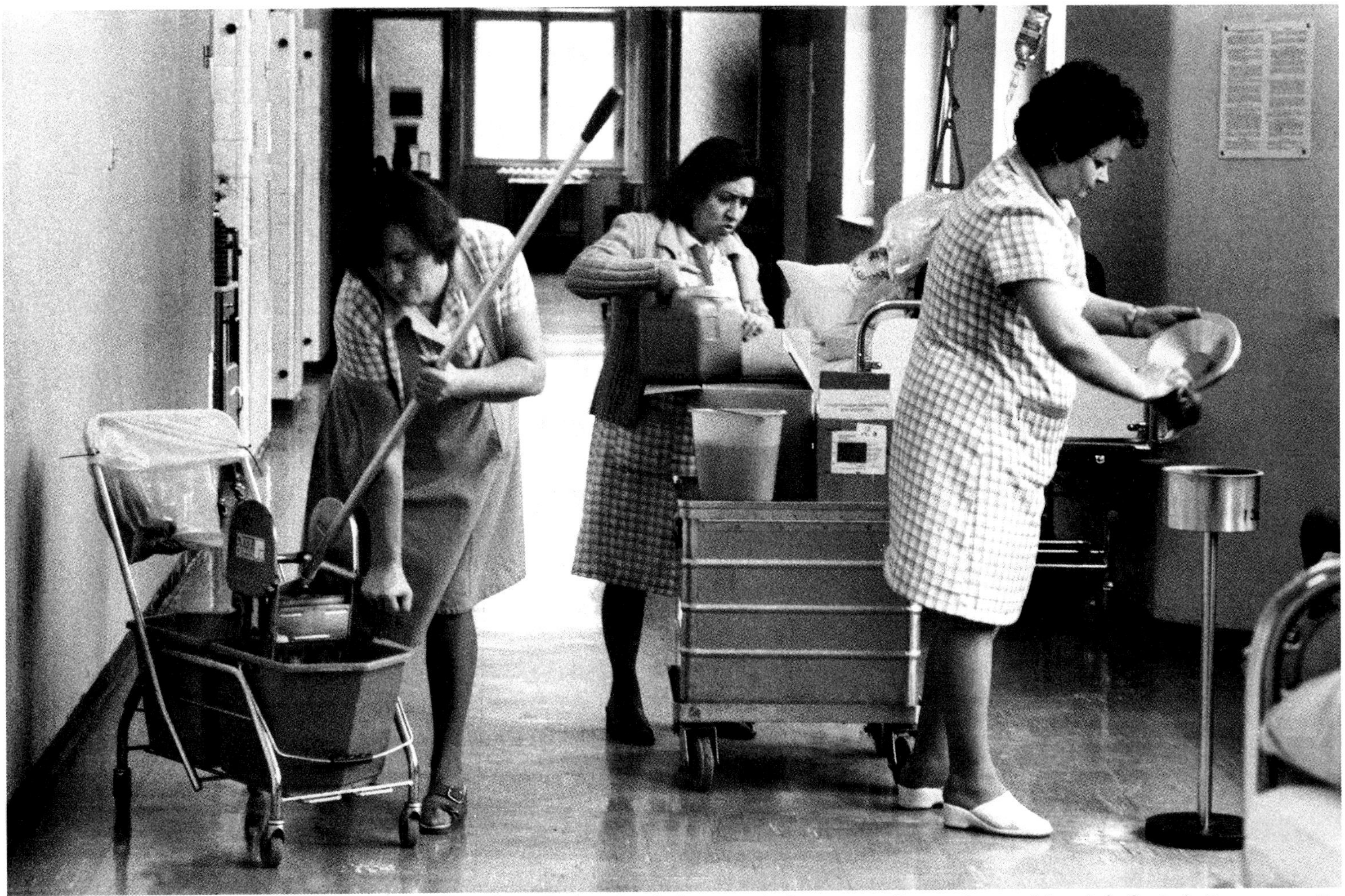

Cleaners at a hospital in Schwabing—from left, a Yugoslav, a Turk and an Italian—typify the cosmopolitan make-up of the city's Gastarbeiter community.

A multinational gang of navvies, some equipped with ear-muffs to blot out the noise of their pneumatic drills, carry out repairs to Munich's tramway tracks.

Groups of gossiping Turks crowd the concourse of Munich's main railway station, a favoured gathering-place for immigrants since the first foreign workers stepped off the trains to take up jobs in the city. Although by the late 1970s foreign labour was no longer being recruited, a steady influx of illegal immigrants arrive by clandestine means to seek their fortune.

HERTIE

Three young Greeks are photographed by a friend after attending church on a Greek national holiday.

Immaculately dressed baby girls fidget in their mothers' arms after receiving a Greek Orthodox christening at the Church of St. Johann in south Munich.

At Munich's mosque, built in 1973 with donations from the faithful, a largely Turkish congregation takes part in Friday prayer, high point of the Muslim week.

In an apartment stacked with cherished and expensive electronic gear, a Turk on sick leave from his job at B.M.W. is visited by two compatriots.

MEIN KAMPF
HITLER REDEN

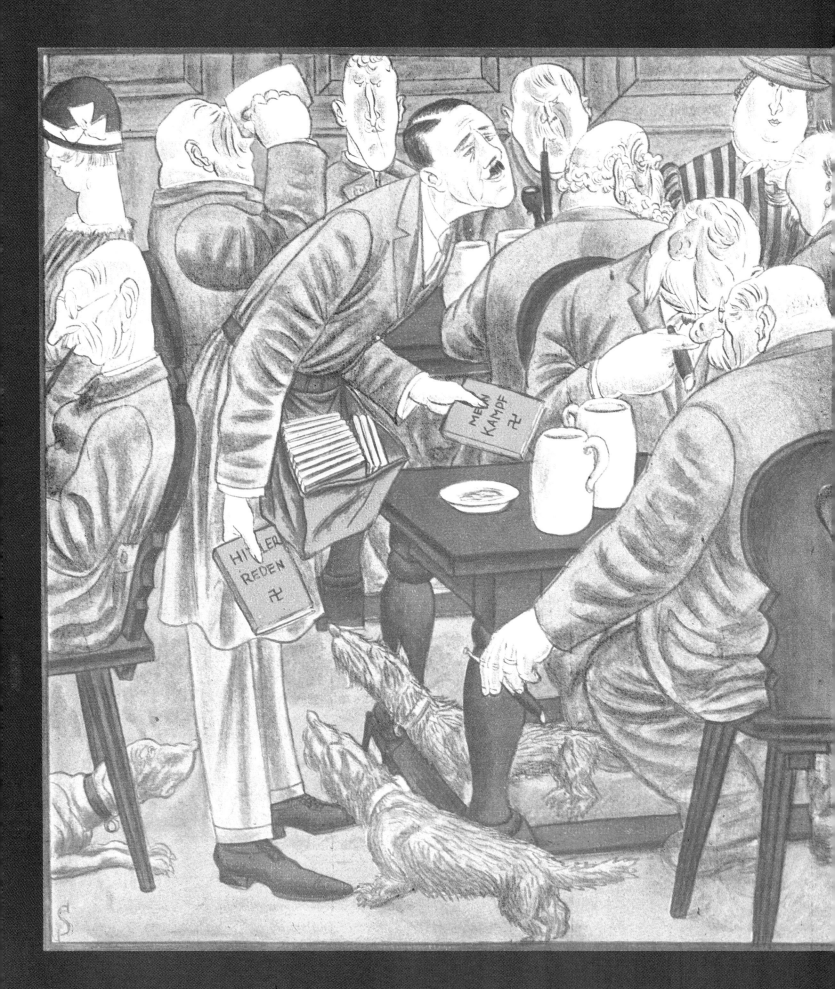

5
The Dark Decades

To most people, at least in the Western world, the word Munich means first and foremost the "Munich crisis" of 1938: the false alarm or dress rehearsal for the outbreak of the Second World War that brought the French and British leaders to the Bavarian capital for a last-minute confrontation with Germany's Chancellor Adolf Hitler and Italy's Mussolini. For Munich, besides being a happy Bavarian holiday ground and an historic city of abounding artistic riches, is also a city of political importance—and the place where Hitler's Nazi Party originated and grew into a national force. But Munich's 20th-Century politics are neither simple nor one-sided. Hitler emerged from a time of chaos in that desperate period of Germany's prostration after her defeat in the First World War, when a bewildering succession of Bavarian regimes culminated in a soviet republic that died a violent death. In such a context, the abortive putsch with which the Nazis first came to general notice in 1923 was simply one in a series of escalating attempts on the State: one step in the process by which Munich developed from a comfortable monarchist capital, harbouring all kinds of avant-garde thinkers, into the headquarters of National Socialism.

The year 1918 was one of disaster and uncertainty for Germany. In the summer, the Kaiser's Chief of Staff, General Erich Ludendorff, had promised immediate victory in the West, only to have his massive offensive hammered to a halt by an Allied counter-offensive. The Allies also made progress in the East, forcing Germany's allies, Turkey and Bulgaria, to surrender. Even though the Western Front remained intact, Germany—threatened on both flanks—faced imminent defeat. In October, Germany and Austria-Hungary sued for peace. But a condition imposed by the Allies was the resignation of the Kaiser and the Austro-Hungarian Emperor—an end, in effect, to the Hohenzollern and the Habsburg monarchies—and a recognition of the independence of the Polish, Hungarian, Czech and other Slav minorities within the Austro-Hungarian and German empires. Ludendorff resigned. By early November, with collapse threatening, Germany's socialist parties—both the majority Social Democratic Party or Majority Socialists and a new extremist splinter group, the Independent Socialists—were in a frenzy, believing that the end of all European monarchies was near and an era of social democracy was dawning. For their part, the Communists saw the imminent coming of the revolution that had been predicted by Marx, and was already a reality in Russia.

Munich reflected these events and emotions in its own way. The Bavarians—militarily and diplomatically part of the Reich, but independent

In this cartoon of 1924 from the Munich-based magazine "Simplicissimus", Adolf Hitler peddles copies of his political speeches and his autobiography "Mein Kampf" (My Struggle) to beer-hall customers. The Nazi leader had just been released from eight months' imprisonment for his part in the abortive putsch against the Bavarian government the year before.

in their local administration, and more so in character—were weary of war, bitter about what they saw as the failure of Prussian leadership, and utterly confused about what the future might hold. A new, 200,000-strong workforce, built up to man Munich's wartime industries, had created an unprecedented proletarian political dimension. The monarchy was unpopular as an institution, although the mild-mannered King Ludwig III was not personally disliked. Would the Allies negotiate a separate peace with Bavaria? Would they negotiate with Ludwig? If so, would the Majority Socialists, a growing power since they entered the Bavarian Parliament in 1899, agree? Should Bavaria preserve her links with Berlin? Or break away to reassert her independence? Early that November, nothing was certain; anything—from the continuation of a firm monarchist government backed by the army to a Communist uprising—seemed possible.

In Munich, the man who seized the opportunity provided by the moment was a Jewish journalist named Kurt Eisner, a small man with steel-rimmed glasses, a scraggy beard and long wisps of hair edging his bald pate. Born in Berlin in 1867, Eisner had come to Munich in 1910 and had rapidly made himself the city's dominant socialist intellectual. In 1917, he became a founder member of the extreme left-wing Independent Socialist Party in Germany, and leader of the tiny Munich branch. In the autumn of 1918, as defeat stared the country in the face, he decided to take action. In early November, joined for the occasion by the Majority Socialists, he organized a massive demonstration for peace, carefully ensuring that two dozen disaffected returned soldiers would be on hand to back him up.

On the afternoon of Thursday, November 7, some 50,000 people converged on the Theresienwiese. As pre-arranged, a number of returned soldiers emerged from the crowd and gathered round Eisner. They called upon others to join them. Soldiers poured from the mob; then, with Eisner at their head, they sacked their own barracks and scattered into the town. The Bavarian government was without troops and could do nothing. Between 8 and 9 p.m. that evening, Ludwig III and the rest of the royal family drove out of Munich and fled over the border into Austria—thus ending 738 years of Wittelsbach rule.

That very same hour, Eisner organized workers and soldiers in the city's largest beer cellar, the Mathäserbräu, just off the Karlsplatz. Then, escorted by an armed guard of 60 troopers and a crowd of workers, he arrived at the Parliament building, took the Speaker's chair and at 10.30 p.m. proclaimed the establishment of a Bavarian republic. By morning, the city was plastered with bright red posters proclaiming the new order. Revolution had come, and without a single serious casualty.

Events in Bavaria were paralleled by developments in Prussia. On November 9, two days after Eisner's declaration, the Majority Socialists in Berlin, eager to pre-empt the possibility of an uprising by the extreme Left, proclaimed Germany a republic. The Kaiser fled to Holland. On Monday,

Socialist revolutionary Kurt Eisner instigated the November 1918 insurrection that toppled the Bavarian monarchy, ending more than 700 years of Wittelsbach rule and contributing to Germany's post-First World War era of chaos. Eisner proclaimed a socialist republic with himself as premier, but was not returned to office in the subsequent election. Early in 1919 he was assassinated by a young nationalist.

November 11, the new Socialist government signed the Armistice. It was the end of the war, and the end of an era.

But it was by no means clear that another era had dawned. Soldiers, still armed and uniformed, headed for the big cities, tired, unemployed, penniless, some eager for a return to the military ideals for which they had fought, others disillusioned and alienated from those ideals. In Berlin, the new Social Democratic government was scarcely in power before it was besieged. In January 1919, an uprising by the extreme left-wing Spartacist group—precursors of the German Communist Party—was joined by the Independent Socialists, but ended brutally when right-wing troops, part of a paramilitary force known as the Freikorps, captured and murdered the leaders, Rosa Luxemburg and Karl Liebknecht.

Under the impact of the violence in Berlin, politics in Munich polarized. Extremists were active everywhere, from Communists and anarchists such as the idealistic Schwabing poet and cabaret performer Erich Mühsam, to monarchists such as the members of the extreme right-wing Thule Society, many of whose members later became leading Nazis. The Independent Socialist Eisner was attacked on every hand. Conservatives vilified him as an outsider, an intellectual, a Jew, a Bolshevik; Communists accused him of not going far enough. In a spate of revolutionary fervour, workers and soldiers established some 7,000 local councils—*Räte*, or soviets, as they were known. The local groups were responsible to a Central Soviet, but this body had no formal connection with the Eisner government.

Eisner, short on parliamentary experience and solid political support, could rule only with the backing of the Majority Socialists, led by Erhard Auer, who repeatedly demanded elections. Eisner had little choice but to comply. For his Independent Socialists the results, declared in mid-January, were disastrous: the Majority Socialists won easily, while Eisner received a derisory $2\frac{1}{2}$ per cent of the vote. Facing the inevitable, he prepared to resign, but he never got a chance to do so.

On the way to announce his resignation on February 21, Eisner was shot dead by a fanatically nationalistic young aristocrat, Count Anton von Arco Valley. The Eisner murder was immediately followed by a second attack, which many saw as an attempted revenge killing. In the Parliament Building shortly after the announcement of Eisner's death, a butcher named Alois Lindner ran into the assembly, pulled out a gun and shot Auer, severely wounding him. Lindner then shot dead two others who tried to bar his way, and escaped.

With Eisner gone, there was no unifying socialist figure. The new Majority Socialist leader, Johannes Hoffmann, had the authority neither of Eisner nor of the grievously wounded Auer. The Communists took matters into their own hands, and initiated a month of chaos. On April 4, soviet delegates trudged through 20 inches of snow to a huge meeting in the Löwenbräukeller, where they proclaimed the first soviet republic. Rather than face these hard-liners, Johannes Hoffmann, the new premier of the official socialist administration—the Whites, as they came to be known—retired to Bamberg, north of Nuremberg, stating loudly that he was still in office. Bavaria was on the way to its own miniature civil war.

The soviet leaders—left-wing intellectuals all, with not a worker among them—operated incongruously from the panelled and gilded halls of the Wittelsbach Residenz. These inexperienced leaders proved totally inadequate for the task of government. Some were impractically idealistic, others were downright eccentric. The poet Mühsam announced the transformation of the world "into a meadow full of flowers in which each man can pick his share", and ordered poetry to be printed alongside the revolutionary decrees. The Minister for Foreign Affairs, Franz Lipp, sent a telegram to Lenin in Moscow complaining angrily that Hoffmann had stolen the keys to the ministry washroom; Lenin forbore from involving himself in the dispute. One of the Red leaders, Ernst Toller, a Jew, future playwright and at that moment the well-intentioned President of the Central Soviet, recorded how "all day long people crowded into the ante-room, waiting their turn to see me. Each one of them believed that the Soviet Republic had been expressly created to satisfy his own private desires. A woman wanted to get married at once. . . . A man wanted his landlord to remit his rent. . . . Unappreciated cranks submitted their programmes for the betterment of humanity. . . . Some believed that the root of all evil was cooked food, others the gold standard, others unhygienic underwear, or machinery, or the lack of a compulsory universal language."

Another weakness in the new regime was that a number of hard-line Communists in the city were uncompromising in their desire for full control. Dominated by two men with surprisingly similar names—Max Levien and Eugen Leviné, both of whom had been sent in by Communists in Berlin—the hard-liners refused to share power with such a peculiar mixture of socialists, idealists and anarchists.

Then, to cap it all, the White leader Hoffmann sent in his own republican security troops from Bamberg to depose the soviets. This was the chance the hard-line Communists had been waiting for. On April 13 at the Hofbräuhaus, workers and soldiers elected Leviné as the head of the Second—the "true"—Soviet Republic, appointing the Hofbräuhaus as their government headquarters. Thus began two weeks of even greater chaos. The Reds at once issued thousands of weapons to a rabble of townsmen, generously paying the new recruits in advance. But the Red Army was as feckless as its leaders; drunkenness was rife in the ranks and discipline almost non-existent, as many of the troops simply pocketed their pay and at the first opportunity returned home. The independent peasant farmers greeted the Communists with contempt and refused to supply food.

The end came rapidly and violently. The anti-Communist Hoffmann requested intervention by Berlin and a force of 20,000 troops was sent

A 1919 election poster graphically puts forward the point of view of the conservative Bayerische Volkspartei (Bavarian People's Party) urging voters to resist the fiery message of Bolshevism being taken to Munich by Berliner Kurt Eisner, leader of the extreme left-wing Independent Socialists. The election, in January of that year, was held to choose representatives for the Bavarian Republic's first parliament after the November 1918 insurrection overthrowing the monarchy. The election was a victory for the moderately left-wing Majority Socialist Party.

BERLIN
MÜNCHEN
II/6
BAYERN, DER BOLSCHEWIK GEHT UM!
HINAUS MIT IHM AM WAHLTAG!
BAYERISCHE VOLKSPARTEI

Members of the Red Army, a German volunteer force formed to defend the second of the Communist-led Bavarian soviet republics in April 1919, gather outside Munich's railway station. Their government lasted for almost a month—until the volunteers were wiped out by troops brought in from Berlin by the ousted administrators of the legal socialist republic.

towards Munich. In the countryside outside Munich, another anti-Communist army was preparing itself—the Bavarian arm of the Freikorps. Within a few days, Munich was surrounded by 35,000 troops. Both sides began to take hostages. The Whites, as they closed in, dealt out summary "justice"—they shot 50 Red captives. In retaliation, the soviets, holding hostages in the Luitpold Secondary School, shot 10 of their prisoners.

By May 2, the city was in White hands again. The revenge killings went on until hundreds more had died. Hoffmann was restored at the head of a Social Democratic government. Leviné was captured, later condemned to death and executed. Ernst Toller got off with a prison sentence, as did Mühsam. Both, however, later died violent deaths: Mühsam in 1934 after repeated beatings in a Nazi concentration camp, Toller by his own hand in New York in 1939, in despair at the coming of war.

The whole interlude from the departure of the Wittelsbachs to the comparative stability under Hoffmann's reinstalled Social Democratic government had taken place within only six months, between November 1918 and May 1919. The violent episode of the soviets had lasted less than 30 days. But the events made a deep impression on Münchners—and, in particular, on Adolf Hitler. The young Austrian had come to the city from Vienna in 1913, and had been delighted by its tolerance of artistic eccentricity and political extremism. He had joined a Bavarian regiment in 1914, had served with some distinction and had suffered temporary blindness as a result of a gas attack at the end of the war. Recovered by late 1918, he was ordered to report back to his regimental barracks in Munich. He was appalled by what he found. When he arrived at the end of November at the

A Bavarian unit of the Freikorps, a right-wing militia, assemble for a group portrait in 1919. Some 15,000 Freikorps troops, including many former German Army officers, converged on Munich to join forces with the defenders of the legal socialist government, defeating the Communist regime that had briefly held power.

Türkenstrasse barracks near Schwabing, he was shocked—or so he later asserted—to see the place in the hands of a soldiers' soviet. To him, the Jews and Reds had taken over. The army itself, the guardian of the ideals of the Reich, seemed infected with Communism. Horrified by such goings on, he immediately requested, and obtained, a winter posting doing guard duty at a P.O.W. camp on the Austrian frontier.

Hitler returned to Munich in February 1919, in time to witness the chaos that followed Kurt Eisner's assassination and the rule of the soviets, experiences that only intensified his determination to reverse the humiliation of defeat and eradicate the influence of his own particular *bêtes noires*, the Jews and the Bolsheviks.

Moreover, Hitler felt himself to be on firm ground. He was born in the Austrian town of Braunau am Inn, in an area that had been part of Bavaria until the 18th Century. He spoke with the characteristic South German accent. And he shared the interests of the strongest, most disaffected social group in Germany—the mass of demobbed soldiers, rootless, unemployed and violent. They had fought hard and well for their country. Now, with the army limited to 100,000 by the Treaty of Versailles, signed in June 1919, they were without a future. Those who longed for a return to military values formed private bands—the Freikorps was only one example among many—that bivouacked around Munich, making a force that promised stability after the disorder left by the soviets and encouraging the notion, common among Bavarian officers and monarchists, that Bavaria could become a fortress from which all Germany could be ruled.

Hitler was among the lucky ones. He was still in the regular army, and was assigned a job with the local press and news bureau of the army's political department. In this capacity, he was called upon to look into the activities of a tiny nationalistic political group calling itself the German Workers' Party. In September 1919, he became a member. This was to be his political springboard. In July 1921, he took over the party, which by that time had prefaced its name with the all-important words "National Socialist"—*Nationalsozialistisch* or Nazi for short.

The four years from 1919 to 1923 were utterly disastrous for Germany. The Treaty of Versailles sliced off parts of the country and imposed crippling reparations. Germany simply did not have the money, and suspended payments. To enforce the treaty terms the French, in January 1923, occupied the industrial Ruhr area. To keep up the resumed payments, Germany printed more and ever more marks, a step that led to galloping inflation. By November 1923, matters had reached such an extreme that it took four million million marks to equal one U.S. dollar.

Bavaria responded to these events in its own way. In March 1920, Johannes Hoffmann's Social Democratic government resigned, and was replaced by a right-wing government under Gustav von Kahr, a local politician who had monarchist leanings, and who was backed by army commander Otto von Lossow and State Police Chief Hans von Seisser. This triumvirate was determined to reassert Bavaria's traditional autonomy and resurrect, if possible, a firm patriotic government.

This suited Hitler admirably. Kahr saw Hitler as a potential ally who could win the workers' support; for his part, Hitler had been cultivating the aging General Ludendorff, who had come to live outside Munich, as a possible military figurehead.

Then, in 1922, an event occurred that acted as an inspiration to Hitler: Mussolini's March on Rome, by which the Fascists seized control in Italy. Hitler, now well-known locally as a rising politician, hoped for similar success in Germany—a march from Munich to Berlin leading to a revolution that would catapult him to power.

He now had the organization to accomplish his aims. Since he had joined the German Workers' Party in 1919, he had been developing his own peculiar political style. As was traditional in South Germany, meetings were almost always held in beer cellars, chiefly the three largest in Munich—the Hofbräuhaus, the Löwenbräukeller and the Bürgerbräukeller. Here, to audiences of anything from a dozen to more than a thousand, he would denounce the Jews, the government in Berlin and the Communists, recall in tough working-class dialect the sacrifices of the war, and promise instant remedies. His swaggering brown-shirted bully-boys, the Storm Troopers, stood ready to silence any opposition and to shout their agreement to each point Hitler made.

Towards the end of 1923, as the great inflation gathered momentum, Hitler saw his chance. He suspected the crisis would lead the Munich triumvirs to break completely with Berlin, thus ending his hopes of using

Bavaria as a springboard for a national revolution. To forestall them he determined on his own seizure of power in Munich.

On November 8, 1923, Kahr, Lossow and Seisser held a meeting for 3,000 civil servants and businessmen in the Bürgerbräukeller in the district of Haidhausen across the river from the city centre. Kahr was well into his speech when Hitler, proudly displaying on his black tailcoat the military Iron Cross he had won in the war, forced his way into the main hall, waving a pistol. With the doorways blocked by Storm Troopers—one group of them with a machine-gun—Hitler marched to Kahr's side. A shot was fired at the ceiling. As silence fell, he shouted: "The national revolution has begun!" and ordered the government leaders into a neighbouring room. There, he demanded that they join him in his revolution. They refused. Hitler went back into the hall to address the crowd. As always when he spoke, he electrified his audience. To onlookers the insignificant little man in an ill-fitting morning coat suddenly became the master orator, Germany's saviour. "Either the German revolution begins tonight," he raved, "or we will all be dead by dawn." The crowd cheered ecstatically.

Meanwhile, Hitler had dispatched an envoy to fetch General Ludendorff, who knew nothing of the putsch, but testily agreed to come. The arrival of the great General caused Kahr and the others to capitulate. They agreed to show themselves with Hitler and Ludendorff in a demonstration of unity. The crowd again howled its approval, and then dispersed. The Nazis huddled down for the night in the beer cellar, or roamed the damp streets of Munich waiting for the orders that would, they hoped, lead to the subsequent capture of the city.

At once, however, the tide of events began to turn against Hitler. Lossow, claiming that he had supported Hitler only under duress, repudiated the putsch in a statement that was read over the radio. The police were called out in force. Nonplussed, Hitler vacillated; but finally, at midday, he gathered together his disheartened followers, some 2,000 in all, in the Rosenheimerstrasse, near the Bürgerbräukeller. Then with himself and Ludendorff to the fore, the procession marched off. Hitler's purpose was, apparently, to confront the forces of the State with a demonstration of Nazi power, without having a specific military objective in mind.

The Nazis marched over the Ludwigsbrücke, forcing their way through a police cordon, across the Isartorplatz to the Marienplatz and then wheeled right, swinging into the narrow Residenzstrasse. At the end of the street, on the spacious Odeonsplatz, another police cordon blocked their way. There, as the Nazis marched forward in the shadow of the Feldherrnhalle, a single shot rang out—no one knows from which side. There followed a furious 60-second exchange of fire that left 17 dead—14 of them Nazis. The events were confused but, according to one account, one of the dead was a bodyguard who had been walking arm in arm with Hitler. As the bodyguard fell, he yanked Hitler to the ground, dislocating his left shoulder. Hitler tried to flee. Ludendorff, trembling with rage, simply stomped straight ahead into the waiting arms of the police.

Hitler, too, was arrested, and both he and Ludendorff were tried for treason, along with eight others. In court, Hitler turned disaster into triumph, insisting on taking responsibility for the putsch, and rejecting the charge of treason. "There can be no question of treason," he claimed histrionically, "in an action which aims to undo the betrayal of this country in 1918. . . . I consider myself not a traitor but a German, who desired what was best for his people." The trial was a sensation, and Hitler became a national figure. Instead of being deported as a foreigner to Austria, Hitler received a technical five-year sentence, with the plain understanding that he would serve only a few months. He spent them in the Landsberg Fortress, 33 miles west of Munich, in a relatively congenial section for political prisoners, and suffered none of the hardships imposed on common criminals. He used his time to write *Mein Kampf* (My Struggle), his account of his path to greatness, which was later to become required reading for all Nazis.

On his release, Hitler was confronted with a party in ruins. He not only had to rebuild it, he also had to break out of Bavaria. Munich, used to artistic and political eccentricity, might simply have absorbed his movement, killing it with tolerance. Hitler knew that to achieve power nationally he would have to establish himself in Berlin. And that goal he successfully accomplished, with ruthless determination and demagogic skill, in the eight years between December 1924, when he was released from Landsberg, and January 1933, when he became Chancellor.

At first, progress was slow. For Germany, the years from 1925 to 1929 brought relative stability. Reparations payments were reduced to a more realistic figure. The economy began to recover from the ravages of the great inflation. The republic seemed secure. In its new President, Paul von Hindenburg, the grand old man of Germany's armed forces, it acquired a symbol of authority and stability. During these years, Hitler could do little but re-establish his hold on the party, whose membership rose from 27,000 to 178,000 by the end of the decade.

But in 1929 new disaster struck. America and Europe plunged into economic depression. The German export market collapsed. Factories closed. Banks crashed. Millions were thrown out of work.

And Nazism thrived. In the parliamentary elections of 1930, the Nazis won 107 seats, second only to the Majority Social Democrats. In July 1930, Hitler was able to use 1.5 million marks of Nazi funds to buy a hundred-year-old palace at Briennerstrasse 45—between Karolinenplatz and Königsplatz—as the Nazi Party national headquarters. He renamed the building the Brown House, identifying it with the Nazis' favourite colour. The Brown House rapidly became the nerve-centre of a nationwide party

On November 9, 1933, Germany's new Chancellor Adolf Hitler (centre) strides through Munich in the first annual commemoration of the putsch of 1923.

bureaucracy; an embryonic alternative to the administration in Berlin. In 1932, Hitler challenged Hindenburg in the presidential elections, and did well. In the parliamentary elections of January 1933, the Nazis more than doubled their strength to win 230 seats, the largest block, though not an overall majority. Hitler was offered the chancellorship, and accepted.

After he became Chancellor, Hitler spent most of his time in Berlin, but his attachment to Munich continued throughout the 1930s. The city was given the title *Hauptstadt der Bewegung* (Capital of the Movement)—a legend that appeared on its Third Reich postmark. There were Nazi uniforms everywhere, and at the Feldherrnhalle, converted to a Nazi shrine in memory of those who fell in the 1923 putsch, a permanent SS guard exacted the Nazi salute from all passers-by. This being Munich, however, many could not stomach the arrangement: to avoid the salute, some Münchners preferred to cut round the back of the monument, along a small street, Viscardigasse, which became known as "Slacker Street".

Every two or three weeks Hitler came on well-publicized visits to Munich, where he had a nine-room apartment at Prinzregentenplatz 16. In the mountains above the village of Berchtesgaden, 76 miles south-east of the city, a large comfortable chalet was built to Hitler's own design as a retreat to which foreign diplomats and visitors were sometimes invited. The Führer made a point of being in the city each November 8, the anniversary of the putsch, when celebrations began in the Bürgerbräukeller.

Indeed, Hitler set about physically remaking the city in a style in keeping with its historic status as the birthplace of Nazism. His love of architecture would have found as massive expression in Munich as it did in Berlin and Nuremberg had not many of his grandiose schemes been overtaken by the outbreak of the Second World War. He wanted monuments to his revolution, and they were to be "nationalist" in style: huge halls, stadiums, amphitheatres and neoclassical arcades, with heavy decorations, rows of thickly framed windows, and friezes extolling labour, motherhood or military might. For Munich, two new, 130-yard-wide avenues were planned, one scything east from a new railway station across the Isar, the other north from the existing station near the Theresienwiese. Much of old Munich was to be destroyed. Schwabing was to be redesigned and two new cities —"ideal" Nazi communities—were to be built to the north and south.

In 1935, a start was made with the Königsplatz, which was to be the jewel in Munich's Nazi crown. Its extensive lawns vanished, to be replaced by 26,000 square yards of granite slabs brought from the Black Forest, turning it into a grandiose altar to the New Order. The first autobahns were built, radiating from Munich in the directions of Salzburg, Berlin and Garmisch-Partenkirchen, where the 1936 Winter Olympics were held; and an underground railway was planned.

The three major Nazi buildings that chanced to survive destruction in the war were the House of German Art, now known simply as the House

At the head of the table, Adolf Hitler relaxes in 1932 with Nazi friends after taking part in a party meeting in Munich's Hofbräuhaus. Because it had been the site of the first large-scale meeting of the embryonic party in 1920, the main hall of the Hofbräuhaus—capable of holding 2,000 people—was a favourite forum for Nazi rallies.

of Art, the Führerbau (Hitler's own office) and the neighbouring Nazi administration centre. The latter two are rarely mentioned in guidebooks, and now house respectively the state's College of Music and Institute of Culture. All were designed by Paul Ludwig Troost, who was Hitler's chief architect until his death in 1934.

The Führerbau stands almost on the Königsplatz, where Arcisstrasse meets Briennerstrasse. Together with its sister building, the Nazi administration centre, it replaced the Brown House as the party headquarters. The three-storey house is built of yellow Danubian limestone; its massive balcony, jutting from beneath the picture-frame windows on the second floor and supported by eight fluted columns, still acts as a reminder of its intended use: as a stand from which to review parades and make speeches.

Inside, two marble stairways, flanked by pillars, lead up from the 65-foot-high hall to a living room, a dining room, a great semicircular hall, and Hitler's own office, all of them wood-panelled, decorated with marble, and boasting huge marble fireplaces. Strangely, after the war, this building was briefly used as America House, the local cultural headquarters of the United States, until new headquarters were established in its present building round the corner on the Karolinenplatz.

The House of Art, which overlooks the southern fringe of the English Garden, is a 190-yard-long sandstone building, whose façade of heavy pillars epitomizes the neoclassical style beloved by Hitler. The Führer himself laid the cornerstone on October 15, 1933, tapping it ceremonially with a silver hammer. The hammer broke. Hitler later claimed to have seen this event as an evil omen, which he believed was fulfilled when, four months later, the architect Troost died. The gallery's opening in 1937 was marked by an exhibition of "degenerate art" organized by Dr. Goebbels, including pictures by Impressionist and Expressionist painters of whom the Nazis disapproved. The intention was to hold the works up to ridicule; but, when it became apparent that the modernist paintings were exciting far greater public interest than the approved social-realist exhibits elsewhere in the gallery, the exhibition was prematurely closed.

After 40 years, there is little today that would identify the building with its Third Reich origins. Its exhibitions of modern art are internationally admired, and all obvious traces of Nazism have long since been removed —except that on the ceiling of the long porch, behind the colonnade of pillars, are the original red and green tiles, patterned into stylized swastikas.

One other construction of the 1930s rapidly acquired the most appalling of reputations: the concentration camp at Dachau, a little suburban township 10 miles north of Munich until then noted mainly for its artistic community. The Dachau camp, set up in 1933, was the first such camp to be opened in Germany; by the end of that year there were more than 50. Mostly, the camps were used by the Storm Troopers to mete out beatings to political opponents such as Mühsam, who met his death there. But in 1934 Hitler handed over the control of the camps to the SS, which proceeded to organize them with ruthless efficiency. SS guards, with their skull-and-crossbones insignia, were from the feared Death's Head unit; the SS commander, Theodor Eicke, was also commander of Dachau. Although Dachau was not built as an extermination camp, at least 31,000 people are recorded as having died there, and it was the scene of Dr. Sigmund Rascher's "medical" experiments on human toleration of extreme conditions such as very low temperatures.

The camp has been preserved; its wire fences, bleak parade-ground, wooden huts and crematory ovens—the ghastly stench of which used to carry as far as Munich—stand as overwhelming reminders of a horror known to most people only from films and books. It is something of a shock to newcomers to see, only a 20-minute drive from the city, the name "Dachau" on a sign pointing down a sliproad on the autobahn, or marking a station on the *S-bahn*, the suburban rail network. If you see the sign, my advice is: follow it. For in the camp, restored so minutely that it might have just been built, one is suddenly face to face with the stark terror of a world that seems a million miles from the busy, cheerful streets of Munich.

In 1938, Munich found itself for the first time the centre of attention of the entire world, during the crisis that made its very name synonymous with "appeasement": the policy of giving Hitler his way in the hope that his expansionist urges would be satisfied.

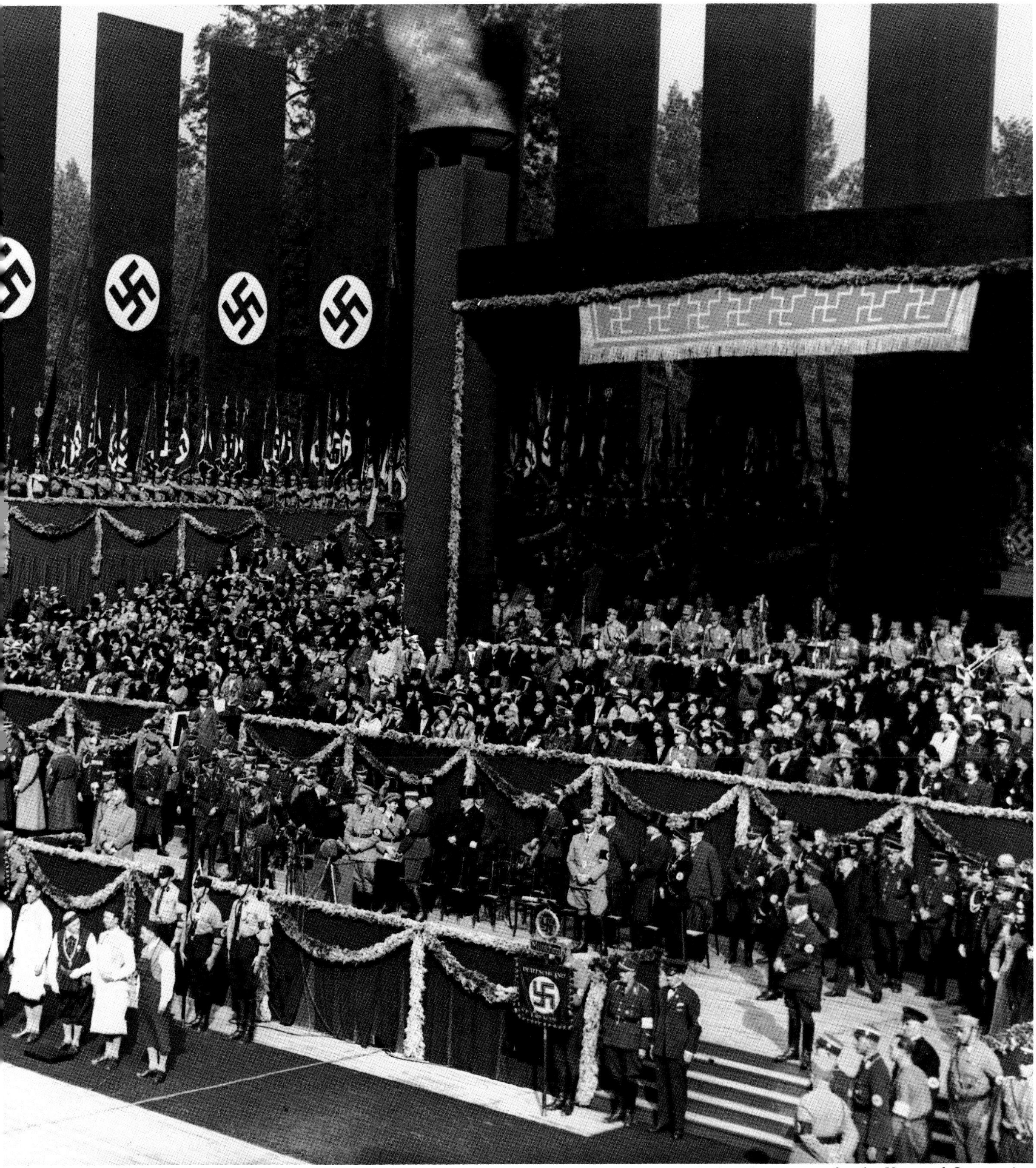

Beneath rows of swastikas, Nazi soldiers and their guests in October 1933 observe the laying of the foundation-stone for the House of German Art.

Hitler's long-term aim was to build a vast new wing to the Third Reich that would include all of Eastern Europe and much of Russia. In March 1938, he annexed Austria, which as a German-speaking nation and his own country of origin he claimed as a natural constituent of his Germanic empire. His next target was Czechoslovakia, which contained a German minority, the Sudetens. For years, its local leaders, egged on by Hitler, had demanded incorporation into the Third Reich. Hitler planned annexation of the Sudetenland as a first step towards the occupation of the whole country, and made it clear that he was ready to fight for the "cause" of the Sudeten Germans. He named October 1 as the deadline by which the area was to be ceded. This was, as it happened, a desperate gamble, for the Germans were not yet prepared for a major war, and France was bound by treaty to come to Czechoslovakia's defence. Moreover, though Britain had no defence treaty with Czechoslovakia, Hitler could not be certain of the British reaction to naked aggression.

In the event, Hitler was given his way, almost entirely through the efforts of Neville Chamberlain, the British Prime Minister. Appalled at the prospect of war, Chamberlain twice flew to Germany in September to negotiate with Hitler, and acknowledged the principle of the "detachment of the Sudeten areas". How was this to be arranged? With a plebiscite, Hitler said, leading to peaceful annexation. Chamberlain won French approval for his plan—only to hear Hitler raise the odds: now he wanted military occupation. The Czechs naturally refused the demand, and mobilized.

During those last few September days before the October deadline, Munich, like the rest of Europe, believed that war was imminent, and nightmarish preparations began. Stations were packed with soldiers being rushed by freight car to the frontiers. The telephones at all the embassies jangled incessantly as anxious foreigners asked frantically for advice and information. The roads were crowded with tourists heading for the border.

On September 27, however, four days before Hitler's deadline, Chamberlain made a final appeal for a peaceful solution. Hitler responded with an invitation to Britain, France and Italy to a conference with him in Munich —the choice of place being at Mussolini's suggestion. Czechoslovakia was to be excluded from the conference.

When news of the conference broke, the mood changed dramatically. Munich exulted that the clouds of war had been dispelled. Houses sported tricolours and Union Jacks, and SS regiments were rushed to take up posts to welcome the foreign statesmen. Lights shone through the night in the usually darkened Führerbau, where the conference was to be held. On the morning of September 29, Mussolini came by train; Daladier, the French Prime Minister, and Chamberlain arrived by air at Oberwiesen airfield. Chamberlain, in particular, received a rapturous reception.

After a snack of Moselle wine and sandwiches, the Big Four, with Hitler's interpreter, Paul Schmidt, took their seats at 12.45 p.m. at the round table

During the last winter of the Second World War, from 1944 to 1945, under a sky filled with smoke from an Allied air attack, guards at an exit of Munich's railway station scrutinize the papers of travelling German soldiers. The number of deserters was rapidly increasing at that time.

MÜNCHEN-HBF

In the Hofgarten, just north of the Residenz, floral tokens of remembrance lie beside the effigy of a First World War soldier that forms the centre-piece of Munich's memorial, now commemorating the dead of both world wars.

in Hitler's wood-panelled office. The mood was one of optimism, for the decision to exclude Czechoslovakia had made the result of the conference a foregone conclusion; all that remained was to formalize the arrangements for the transfer of the Sudetenland to Germany. The conference broke for lunch at 3 p.m. and resumed later with the involvement of numerous advisers who thrashed out the wording of the agreement. Although it was dated September 29, it was finally signed shortly after midnight on the morning of the 30th.

There was to be no war over Czechoslovakia. In Britain and France, shame at the ease with which Hitler had been allowed to get his way was outweighed by relief. It was only six months later that the true nature of Hitler's aim became blindingly clear. On March 15, 1939, what remained of Czechoslovakia collapsed, Hitler seizing the west and Hungary the east. Poland, now half encircled by the Third Reich, was to be the next victim. On September 1, the German Army crossed the Polish border and two days later Britain and France declared war.

The war years in Munich, though mostly of significance to the city for the destruction wrought by Allied bombing raids, are also remembered for the short-lived reassertion of Munich's individuality. Here occurred perhaps the most ingenious of the many attempts on Hitler's life, and here too arose a doomed opposition movement—one of the very few in Germany and the only civilian one—known as the White Rose.

The attempt on Hitler's life occurred on November 8, 1939, two months after the outbreak of war. The demonstrators killed in the Munich beer-hall putsch of 1923 had, since 1933, been revered as Nazi martyrs and November 8 had become a high party holiday. There was a rigid protocol for the

Dominating the eastern edge of the Hofgarten, the domed central section of the Bavarian Army Museum, built in 1905, is a gaunt reminder of the intensive bombing raids that Munich experienced during the Second World War.

event, which naturally was held in the Bürgerbräukeller, the scene of the 1923 putsch. The celebration began promptly at 8 o'clock in the evening and half-an-hour afterwards Hitler began his speech, which took at least an hour. But, on the day of the 1939 anniversary, Hitler began speaking at 8.10 p.m.—twenty minutes ahead of schedule—to the crowd of 3,000 party members, finished with one *"Sieg Heil!"* at 9.07 and hurriedly left the scene of his youthful dramas to catch a 9.31 train back to Berlin; the weather was too bad to fly. At 9.20—13 minutes after Hitler had left—a time bomb exploded behind the speaker's platform, killing eight Nazi dignitaries and injuring more than 60 others, one of whom died later.

At the Swiss border, German customs men arrested George Elser, a Swabian cabinet-maker, clock-maker and munitions worker, who subsequently confessed to placing a time bomb in a cavity he had cut in a stone pillar of the Bürgerbräukeller. According to his confession it took Elser 35 nights to complete his formidable task. He hid himself in the beer-hall every night, concealing his work while it was in progress behind the pillar's wood panelling. Elser was held in Dachau until 1945, when he was secretly executed on Gestapo orders.

Elser's motive for attempting to kill Hitler has never been satisfactorily established. It was stated at the time that he planted the bomb because he wanted to prevent war. Subsequently, however, there have been claims that he acted on the instructions of Gestapo agents who wanted, apparently without Hitler's knowledge, to stage a near-miss assassination attempt as a way of boosting popular support for the Führer and the war. Whichever version one accepts, the fact remains that Elser never stood trial.

A little more than three years after the Bürgerbräukeller bombing, on February 12, 1943, shortly after the German disaster at Stalingrad, there appeared on the walls of the University of Munich in large letters in white paint the sign "Down with Hitler!" Leaflets were found throughout the city calling for resistance against the Hitler regime. One leaflet began with the statement: "Nothing is more unworthy of a people of culture than to allow itself to be 'governed' by an irresponsible clique of rulers who indulge the basest instincts." A second leaflet emphasized the fact that "since the conquest of Poland *three hundred thousand* Jews have been bestially murdered in that country. This is the most terrible crime ever committed against the dignity of man, a crime of which no counterpart can be found in the whole of human history." The leaflets were signed by a resistance movement calling itself the "White Rose".

Ten days later, placards in flaming red appeared on the city's walls announcing the arrest, trial and execution of the members of the White Rose—a medical student, Hans Scholl, aged 24, and two other students, Scholl's sister Sophie, 21, and Christoph Probst, 24. Shortly after, in a second trial, Professor Kurt Huber, professor of Psychology and Philosophy, and two more medical students, Willi Graf, aged 25, and Alexander Schmorell, 26, were found guilty of treason and executed.

At her last leave-taking with her parents in prison, Sophie Scholl said with great determination: "This will make waves!" But as far as we know the White Rose made only one wave. In Hamburg, in the second half of the same year, eight university members of the Hamburg branch of the White Rose were arrested, tried and subsequently either died in concentration camps or were executed.

Meanwhile, throughout the war, Munich was being destroyed. Allied bombing of the city began in November 1940, and peaked in 1944, in April, in July and again in December. It then decreased in intensity but continued to the very end of the war. All in all, there were 71 Allied air raids on Munich, as a result of which 10,600 buildings (a sixth of the total, including 30 per cent of the city's housing) were destroyed and 550,000 people left homeless. By the time the war was over, Munich's population had been cut almost in half, to 480,000. Curiously, only about 6,500 people were killed in the bombing; the city never suffered the devastating fire-bomb raids that killed 50,000 people over one nine-day period in the city of Hamburg in 1943, and left at least 35,000 Dresdeners dead in a single February night towards the end of the war in 1945.

One Münchner who recorded something of those terrible years was Wilhelm Hausenstein, art critic and writer, who first came to Munich as a student in 1903. During the war, he lived in Tutzing, 21 miles south-west of Munich, and made many visits into the stricken city. In October 1943, he noted the intensification of bombing raids.

"October 6. Into the town yesterday. Everywhere dust in the air, still not settled after two days, and that certain sweet smell of burnt carrion. The

Opera's walls still stand, but it seems completely burnt out. Above the upper triangular pediment with its scorched mosaic hung a long strip of tin from the roof, like a flag marking the devastation. At the northern end of the Residenz, towards the gardens, bad damage to the west wing, the ochre paintwork torn away to reveal the inflamed, feverish red of the bare wall. A modern city cannot, it seems, produce noble ruins: in most places, it looks like a refuse heap.

"May 1, 1944. Two-thirds of Munich's monuments destroyed.... In ruins or burnt out or seriously damaged are the Palais Leuchtenberg (hit three times); the Odeon—the most beautiful concert hall I have ever seen; the State Library; the neo-Gothic Maximilianstrasse; the Peterskirche; the old Rathaus; both Pinakotheks; the Maximilianeum. What will go next time? A communal possession of the West lies in ruins."

To me, as I look around at the modern city humming with life, at its beautiful buildings glowing again with fresh paint, its comfortable crowds ambling along the streets, its sparkling shop windows, it seems almost impossible to believe it is the same place as that scene of utter destruction I myself witnessed on my arrival in 1945.

Munich has grafted its present back on to its past so successfully that almost no sense of disruption or discontinuity exists: it is again the city that was the Wittelsbach capital, and the home of the "Schwabylonians". There is little to recall the years between the wars, and since 1979 there has been even less. In that year, with a minimum of publicity, the city demolished the Bürgerbräukeller to make room for a new shopping centre.

An Olympian Show-Place

PHOTOGRAPHS BY ASHVIN GATHA

Schoolchildren admire the view from the observation deck of Olympic Tower, the city's 900-foot telecommunications mast that dominates the park.

Selection of Munich as the site for the 1972 Olympic Games inspired the most ambitious planning project in the Bavarian capital's modern history. More than a square mile of undeveloped land north of the city centre was transformed into a vast sports complex, including an open-air stadium with a capacity for 77,000 and a large precinct—the Olympic Village—to accommodate the visiting athletes. When the Games were over, Olympic Park—planned from the start to be of benefit to Munich's own citizens—took on a new role. The stadium now hosts the city's professional soccer team and the village is a popular housing location. The Olympic Hall is still used for boxing and wrestling and also provides an arena for plays and concerts, neatly turning the original setting for a 16-day event into an enduring municipal asset.

Designed to integrate with the park's landscaping, an 18.5-acre roof of acrylic glass covers the Olympic Hall, the pools and part of the main stadium.

A rigid web of translucent tiles hangs from one of the 48 support pylons.

Afternoon shadows lengthen over the rolling terrain surrounding the park's artificial lake. The mounds conceal heaps of rubble from the Second World War.

The telecommunications tower and parts of the roof over the Olympic Hall rise above a landscaped slope.

Tree-lined roads and paths link the park's main stadium (foreground) with the oval velodrome, still in regular use for professional cycling contests.

Plants on roofs and balconies soften the sharp geometry of the tiered apartment blocks in the Olympic Village, built to house the 12,000 athletes from 122 countries who participated in the 1972 Games. The flats are now privately owned or rented out; and the village—with its playgrounds, churches and shopping arcades—has become a populous residential community.

6
World City, Village Ways

Few could have guessed how rapidly Munich would inherit the mantle of Berlin after the war. The city's new significance was brought home to me in 1962 when General Charles de Gaulle went to Munich in the course of a tour of Germany—an historic visit that was the first by a French head of state for almost a century. The tour included visits to the postwar capital, Bonn, and to Cologne and Hamburg. De Gaulle toured the city, took a long look at the Ludwigstrasse and pronounced: *"Voilà une capitale!"*

And a national capital it is, in all but name. Its status is proclaimed by its wealth and by the many facets of its assertive individuality. In every sense of the word, Munich is now a *Weltstadt*, a world city.

The extent to which Munich's physical growth was fuelled by the death of the old Germany is startling. In 1945, when Russia occupied the area that contained Berlin, the zone that later became East Germany, the shattered city was isolated, a capital no longer. Tens of thousands of people fled. Thirty thousand of them came to Munich, which had suffered less than other centres, such as Hamburg and Frankfurt. Between 1945 and 1950, the city's population rose by 50 per cent.

With the influx of people came new businesses and even whole factories. Munich's economy boomed. Siemens, the largest electrical engineering group in Europe, transferred the bulk of its operation from Berlin and East Germany to Munich and Bavaria. The Moosach area in northern Munich is dominated by the massive Maschinenfabrik Augsburg-Nürnberg—better known by its distinctive M.A.N. initials, which appear on the grilles of its trucks. On the Petuelring, two miles north-west of the centre, stands the spectacular, four-tower, high-rise headquarters of the Bavarian Motor Works—B.M.W. Famous before the war for the quality of its cars, B.M.W. was slow to recover after 1945, trailing behind Mercedes and Volkswagen in sales. Now B.M.W. products are again chic the world over.

Here, too, are all the famous names in German aeroplane construction—Dornier, Junkers, Messerschmitt. On the south-east fringe lies Germany's grandest aerospace concern, Messerschmitt-Bölkow-Blohm (M.B.B.), a component company of Panavia, a joint German-British-Italian venture to build the Tornado multi-role combat aircraft. M.B.B. is also a major manufacturer of the European Airbus, a whole battery of missiles, experimental communications satellites and the manned Spacelab satellite due to be launched by the U.S. Space Shuttle in the mid-1980s.

The new postwar industrial strength, and the economic strength it brought in, amazed not only Münchners but all Germany, so much so that

In the sumptuous surroundings of his Schwabing home and office—an historic building that he rents from a member of the Wittelsbach family—a Munich financial consultant glances through his appointments while his associate hovers discreetly behind.

in 1965 Willi Daume, President of Germany's National Olympic Committee, suggested to Munich's mayor, Hans-Jochen Vogel, that his city should host the 1972 Olympics. It would, he said, cost about $157 million. The city elders liked the idea. There was a good site available—the Oberwiesenfeld—which had been used as a dump for Second World War rubble and was a mere two and a half miles from the city centre. "It was a chance to jump ahead with the development of Munich," one of the councillors recalled later of their decision. It was also a chance to proclaim to the world the truth of General de Gaulle's remark.

In 1966, Munich was chosen to host the Games over three other cities—Detroit, Montreal and Madrid. In 1967, a competition for the design of the conversion of the Oberwiesenfeld to an Olympic Park was won by a Stuttgart architect, Professor Günter Behnisch, whose plan was of striking architectural originality.

The most startling of the proposed features was to be the roof, the biggest in the world at the time of its design. But size was not the only consideration: its sweeping tent-like peaks and curves, which were to cover stands in the main stadium and adjoining areas as well, were intended to continue in architectural form the hillocks and vales of the sculptured park landscape, itself a modern reflection of the free-ranging design that had made such a success of Munich's English Garden in the 18th Century. In addition, the roof's covering—on the insistence of the television companies—was to be translucent, to allow through the light needed by the batteries of colour television transmitters, and to avoid the hard shadows that would otherwise have marred coverage of the Games. The challenge of such a concept was formidable. Two hundred and seventy miles of steel hawser, slung from 12 main masts, two of them 260 feet high, and 36 smaller supports, were to hold up almost 18.5 acres of acrylic glass panels—equivalent to the size of 13 American football pitches.

The Olympics had a deeper significance than a mere expression of wealth and artistic exuberance. The Games were intended to erase the stigma on Germany of Hitler's 1936 Olympics in Berlin and on Munich of the infamous 1938 pact. I suspected at the time that one of the reasons the Bavarians were enthusiastic to stage the Games was to prove that they were far better equipped than the martinet Prussians to host such a festival. With coincidental symbolism, the Oberwiesenfeld site had been the airfield where Neville Chamberlain landed for the 1938 Munich conference. Munich intended to prove itself not just a *Weltstadt*, but, as the cliché of the time had it, a *Weltstadt mit Herz*, a "world city with heart", which Berlin most certainly had not been in 1936. These were to be the "cheerful Games", a light-hearted, hail-fellow-well-met occasion.

Quite soon after work began in 1968, the authorities were given an opportunity to show that they really intended to practise what they were preaching. In preparing the ground for the Olympic site, they were con-

One of Munich's 6,000 policemen keeps in touch with his colleagues by walkie-talkie while on duty during a ceremonial occasion in the city centre. His spruce appearance reflects the crisp efficiency in which Munich's police take pride.

fronted with a vexatious problem. In a clearing in a small orchard near a mountain of rubble was a neat, cabin-sized church, 15 feet long and 12 feet wide, built of old lumber, oil cans and other debris.

It had been built by a Russian "holy man" named Timofei Prokorov, a Tolstoy-like patriarch in his eighties, with a full head of long white hair and a flowing white beard. Timofei had been a miner in the Don basin at the outbreak of the Second World War. He claimed that he was hauled off to Austria to provide forced labour by the German Army when they retreated from Russia. Timofei did not return to Russia after the war. Instead, he had a glorious vision in which an angel told him to go to Munich and there build a church. In the 1950s he began construction on the Oberwiesenfeld, using pieces of rubble for building material.

When, in the late 1960s, Timofei refused to make way for Olympic construction, the authorities at first moved to have his church condemned as unsafe. Any other building at such a time and in such a place would have been condemned, if not as unsafe then for some other reason. But a church? Even in this secular day and age, nobody asks a man why he builds a church. After careful deliberation, the city fathers decided to include the tiny church in Olympic Park. It remains in the same place—a monument to God amid the monuments to man. "I was told to build the church and to keep working on it until the Church throughout the world is united," said Timofei after the Games. "I was told to build it here for all the world to see and behold, all the world came!"

What the world found when it got to Munich was everything the planners had hoped and worked for. The steam-hammers were silent, the mud had gone from the roads and ever-changing one-way traffic systems had vanished, the new hotels were completed and Münchners at last saw they had not endured in vain. The city seemed superbly prepared, physically and emotionally, for the invasion of visitors, most of whom—if they had been asked—would surely have agreed with de Gaulle's judgment of 10 years before. With 80 miles of new roadway, 12 miles of suburban railway, with walkways and underpasses, five new luxury hotels and a parking lot for 10,000 cars, Munich was transformed. As one of the mayor's aides said: "We have done 20 years' work in five years."

At last, also, the city had acquired a subway, initially a six-and-a-half-mile system costing $155 million. Hitler had first ordered the building of a subway in 1938 and a half-mile tunnel was bored. But in 1945 the tunnel was "de-Nazified"—it was filled with rubble except for a small section where mushrooms were found growing that was turned into a mushroom farm. Thereafter, the pro-subway lobby was foiled for two decades by the trolley-car lobby. And small wonder, for the street-cars are things of beauty, sleek and quiet. They do not clang, clatter or screech. They purr and glide. Besides, as Munich street-car lovers used to say of their city: "Munich is too beautiful to be traversed in Stygian darkness." But Munich acquired its

Stygian darkness, and getting about the city for both Münchners and Olympic visitors became much easier as a result.

The cost of staging the Games was astronomical. The original estimate had almost quintupled to a final bill of $750 million—more than three times the amount expended on the preceding Mexico Olympics. The cost of the stadium roof alone had shot up by twenty times from an estimate of $3.5 million to a final sum of $63 million. About two-thirds of the sum was met by the sale of television rights and of commemorative coins and by money raised in special lotteries. Of the remaining cost, the city of Munich and the state of Bavaria were to divide half between them, and the federal government was to pay the rest.

As the opening day approached, the horrors of construction and soaring costs receded. The stadium roof looked marvellously ethereal, and also proved to be a masterpiece of engineering, confounding the fears of those who had gloomily predicted it would blow away in the first high wind. The 21-acre Olympic lake, the cycle track, the 14,000-seat indoor sports hall, the five pools in the Swimming Hall, the 4,700 apartments of the Olympic Village—all were ready for the opening of the "cheerful Games".

Yet there was an element of foolhardiness in the determined *bonhomie* with which Munich surrounded the Games. The challenge created by the sudden influx of 600,000 people demanded that good cheer be accompanied by a powerful sense of order and discipline. Considering what followed, it is hardly surprising that Munich's authorities have been criticized for not balancing *Herz* with more solid Prussian efficiency.

The first week passed as cheerfully as anyone could have hoped. At the end of the opening parade of 12,000 athletes, in the shadow of the soaring curves of the stadium's roof, 3,200 Munich schoolchildren sang *"Sumer Is Icumen In"*, a welcome contrast—for those who remembered—to the Nazi anthem, the *"Horst Wessel Lied"*, of Hitler's Olympics. The Games themselves were magnificent. Here pirouetted the glorious little Russian gymnast, Olga Korbut, seizing the hearts of the world. There, on the rostrum, time after time, stood America's Mark Spitz, the hero of the Games, who took seven golds in swimming. All, indeed, seemed golden, until the morning of Tuesday, September 5.

There were, as it appeared later, fatal flaws in the Olympic arrangements. The initial plans to restrict entry into the Olympic Village went by the board when reporters complained of "Gestapo tactics" by the officials. Security round the village—stringent at first—became lax. It became accepted practice for athletes to climb over the village's six-and-a-half foot fence in the small hours after a night on the town. And the Israelis, although fearful of terrorist action by their enemies the Palestinians, were given no greater protection than that accorded to any other participants.

It was not hard for some members of a Palestinian terrorist group to infiltrate the village. They called themselves Black September, after the

One of the most dramatic expressions of Munich's industrial strength, the administrative tower of the huge Bayerische Motorenwerke (Bavarian Motor Works) rises 325 feet above the suburbs of north Munich. Built in 1972, the aluminium tower sports company crests on its summit, a motif repeated on the bowl-shaped structure that houses the B.M.W. museum.

BMW

month in 1970 when Jordan's King Hussein began his campaign to crush the Palestinian guerrillas in his country.

At 4.20 a.m. on September 5, they made their move. Eight of them, well armed, scaled the fence. They headed for the Israeli quarters at Connollystrasse 31, where they killed two athletes and seized nine hostages. By 6 a.m. the police had cordoned off the area. At 9 a.m., the Arabs demanded the release of 200 Arabs imprisoned in Israel and of other terrorists in prison in Germany and Japan. Finally, they demanded a flight out.

The Israeli government steadfastly refused to meet the terrorists' demands. Hours passed, with the whole drama played out in public on television. To break the deadlock, the Germans offered the terrorists a flight from Fürstenfeldbruck airbase, 14 miles to the west. It was a trick: the Germans planned an ambush with sharpshooters. The terrorists accepted.

With hindsight, the planned ambush seemed doomed. To shoot down the eight terrorists, there were only five police sharpshooters (the rest were left to cover the departure from the village). They were instructed to fire whenever the Arabs presented the greatest number of targets—an impossibly vague directive. It was night, and the airfield was ablaze with blinding floodlights that cast confusing stipples of shadow. Nevertheless, one marksman fired, and the others raggedly followed suit. The operation that ensued lasted an hour and a half. Five of the eight Arabs died, and all of the nine hostages were killed by their captors.

Upon these events, tragic enough in themselves, followed more tragedy. Reporters at the airfield gate had picked up rumours that the terrorists had been seized. This, apparently, became magnified into a hoped-for fiction: that the hostages had been rescued. The rumour became "news" and was over-hastily "confirmed" by the Munich police and the government.

It took four hours before the German authorities found the courage to make the facts public. And small wonder: how should one break such terrible news? For the Germans, the tragedy had a particularly ghastly twist. What was supposed to be the turning-point in the country's rehabilitation had turned out an ignominious failure. The most sacred principle involved in the original Olympic Games of ancient Greece was the guarantee of safe passage for all participants. The Germans had failed to provide for the safety of the one people to whom they owed an awesome debt—the Jews.

The horrendous tragedy will never be forgotten—not by Münchners, not by the world. A simple but heartfelt memorial beside Connollystrasse 31 honours the slain athletes with a brief description of how they died and the words "Honour their memory" in German and Hebrew. Yet terrorists and murderers would not be allowed to blot out the message of the Olympics or nullify Munich's Herculean attempt to play host to the world.

Indeed, Münchners one and all recognize the Olympics as a sort of watershed in the development of their city. No one is yet sure if the change is all for the good. One journalist, Claus Heinrich Meyer of the *Süddeutsche*

Members of a Munich street-theatre group give a performance during the international fringe theatre festival held every summer in Olympic Park. The landscaped grounds, just north of the city centre, have now become the established site for many of the city's cultural events.

Zeitung, wrote: "It was as if Munich was chemically purified for the Olympics. Not a speck of dust anywhere. It was polished, and with all the varnishing and veneering, it lost charm." Before the Olympics, Münchners called their city the *Millionendorf*, the village of a million people, a phrase that captured the city's balance between intimacy and internationalism. Today, it is a major world metropolis with the characteristics of bigness everywhere: streets overflowing with traffic, fume-polluted air, and a shortage of housing for its burgeoning population.

It is undeniable, however, that one of Munich's traits now is the wealth of the city—its superb shops, its enormous industry, its well-paid, well-dressed inhabitants. That boom started with the Olympics. In 1972 the cost of living took off. Across the board prices rose by 15 per cent—way above Germany's minimal inflation rate at that time. Property rose by 20 per cent. Some restaurants put up their prices by 40 per cent. Some profited by the boom, others complained. But the prices—and the salaries to match—went on rising faster than anywhere else in Germany.

Perhaps the best way for outsiders to get the measure of Munich's wealth is to see the way the rich eat. Anyone who *is* anyone shops in one of several superb delicatessens—for example, at the legendary Dallmayr in Dienerstrasse, the "Tiffany's of delicatessens" as the *New York Times* once called it, where there are 120 different types of sausage in stock, or at Feinkost Käfer, which arranges the buffets for Munich's most expensive society occasions. From these two emporia, and from the delicatessens in the big

Strolling nonchalantly across the Odeonsplatz, this lissome Münchnerin exemplifies the style and flair for which the city's women have become famous.

stores, aspiring hostesses can buy French chickens fresher than those in Paris and oysters flown daily from the North Sea.

You need to be rich, too, to dine out in Munich's top restaurant, Aubergine, which in 1980 became Germany's only three-star restaurant in the Michelin food guide—indeed one of only two restaurants outside France to be so honoured. It is the place to go if you want the best, and are prepared to spend a minimum of 150 marks (about $80) per head. What you get for that price is sheer magic. Aubergine is small, seating a mere 45 people. It is discreetly and elegantly decorated in a soft lilac, with tables well spaced for easy conversation. Service is flawless. And the cooking is among the best in Europe, thanks to the presiding genius of Eckart Witzigmann, who learnt his craft with the great French chef Paul Bocuse.

No wonder that there are people who consider it the year's greatest luxury to dine there, selecting, perhaps, sweetbreads with asparagus tips and truffles, medallions of sole in paprika cream, and a zabaglione made with champagne and served with a sauce made from fresh strawberries. I have even heard of one American pair whose pleasures were shared vicariously by 19 other couples: they had all contributed $10 to an Aubergine raffle, giving the lucky winners a $200 dinner.

But wealth alone is not character, and it is the city's character that many Münchners fear may be undermined by Munich's postwar opulence. I do not agree. For one thing, the past is, thanks to the postwar policy of restoration, intimately part of the present. And then again, there are a number of traits of the city today that make it unique. Three aspects of its postwar character have struck me especially strongly. First, Munich is the focal point for Bavaria's own intense form of politics, with its formidable leader, Franz Josef Strauss. Secondly, the cinema has become the latest manifestation of Munich's artistic spirit and has won international acclaim. Thirdly, Munich contains a unique mix of separate, if overlapping, communities—both foreign and indigenous.

The politics of Munich and Bavaria have always been apart from the rest of Germany. In the postwar years, the state has assiduously cultivated the idea of its individuality. Schoolchildren are carefully taught that Bavaria is a "free state", and the phrase is constantly reproduced in official publications. The reasons are historical. Like other German states, Bavaria did not abandon its sovereignty when it joined Bismarck's federation in 1871. But, especially proud of its long history of independence, it used the term *Freistaat* in its 1919 Constitution to underline its nominal autonomy. This was retained in its 1946 Constitution, devised before the 1948 Basic Law that applies to West Germany as a whole.

Though the phrase *Freistaat* is an anomaly with no constitutional significance, it does symbolize the sturdy independent-mindedness of the state and its capital. The conservative Christian Democratic Union (C.D.U.)

which rivals the Social Democratic Party (S.P.D.) for national leadership, does not exist in Bavaria. Its place is taken by the state's own Christian Social Union, the C.S.U., which has been in permanent coalition with its big sister since 1949; together, the C.D.U. and C.S.U. form a single parliamentary faction in the Federal Parliament in Bonn.

Though consistently at odds with Munich's left-wing traditions—Munich has been governed by Social Democrats until recently—the Christian Social Union has compiled an impressive record of electoral victories in the rest of Bavaria. In the late 1960s and throughout the 1970s, it has consistently polled 60 per cent or more of the popular vote in the state. Success bred success: in 1978 the party stormed the left-wing bastion of the city government and Munich acquired a Christian Social Lord Mayor.

In 1979 the Christian Social Union took another step forward when it put up its own candidate for West German Chancellor—the brilliant, passionate, tub-thumping, quick-tempered, bull-necked, hated and adored uncrowned king of Bavaria, Munich's own Franz Josef Strauss. He is all that and more, a patchwork of contradictory traits, both personal and political, which arouse equally contradictory responses in his countrymen.

As a student in Munich, he was a member of the Catholic Youth League, an organization suppressed by the Nazis in 1936. He did not join the Nazis, never volunteered for service, and fought only as a conscript. After the war, still in his early thirties, he was appointed a regional director by the American occupation administration and, as a founder-member of the Christian Social Union, was elected a member of the Federal Parliament. He became a minister with responsibility for nuclear energy. Then, as Minister of Defence from 1956 to 1962, he undertook the colossal, controversial task of rearming Germany and integrating the country into the Western Alliance. In 1961 he became chairman of the Christian Social Union.

But success has always been tarnished. His coarse, vituperative manner made him enemies, and in 1962 came a scandal that unseated him. The weekly news magazine *Der Spiegel*, which had constantly sniped at Strauss as a power-hungry warmonger, published supposedly secret details of NATO exercises and claimed that Germany was dismally unprepared for war. The Federal Prosecutor, suspecting treason, had *Spiegel's* offices searched and members of its staff arrested. Strauss was widely held responsible for the Gestapo-style tactics of the police, and had to resign.

He returned home to Munich, apparently finished—only to bounce back four years later, this time as Economics Minister in a coalition government of the two major parties, whose acceptance of Munich's *enfant terrible* amounted to a rehabilitation.

In 1969, when the Christian Democrats lost the election, Strauss went into opposition, a thorn in the flesh of both parties, including the Christian Democrats, his nominal allies. His language has always been violent. He has dismissed leftist demonstrators as "animals to whom you cannot apply

Timofei Prokorov, self-styled Russian holy man, sits in his icon-filled church, built from rubble during the 1950s and now incorporated in Olympic Park.

laws made for humans". He has exhorted Germans to "chase the red rats back where they belong, into their holes". He has sworn at hecklers, bellowing that they were "the best Nazis who ever lived".

Yet Bavarians—and now a majority of Münchners—see his outspokenness as a strength. His faults seem mostly, after all, on the surface. In 1974 and 1978 Bavarians gave him 60 per cent of their votes in the national elections—double the number won by the Social Democrats. In 1979 he became Bavarian Prime Minister and announced he would run for Chancellor. Much to their dismay, the Christian Democrats could find no equally colourful alternative, and were left with little choice but to adopt him. It is hardly surprising that he is seen as the very embodiment of Bavaria and Munich: rip-roaring, assertive, individualistic.

In cinema, the Americans, the Italians, the British, the French have all had their years of international acclaim. The late 1970s saw the rise of the Germans, particularly of directors from Munich. Before that, German cinema had been moribund. The rise of Nazism and the war had shattered the creativity that had characterized Berlin in the 1920s and early 1930s. Even in the immediate postwar years, when Berlin's importance as a film centre was being challenged by other major West German cities, a number of factors—the growth of television, a predilection for soft porn, a spate of banal international co-productions—combined to ensure a low reputation. American-made movies dominated German cinemas.

Then, in 1965, Volker Schlöndorff's *The Young Torless*, made in Munich, signalled the beginning of the revolution. Fifteen years later, Schlöndorff's *The Tin Drum*, also a Munich production, won an Oscar for the Best Foreign Film, the ultimate proof that German films were re-establishing the position they had held half a century before.

Munich is the natural centre for the revival. It has its long tradition of artistic patronage, the receptivity to tolerate and inspire individualists and the capability to handle the products. Of Germany's distributors—some one hundred in all—more than 40 are in Munich, as are two-thirds of the country's studios and production companies. The Bavaria Film Studio, set six miles south of the centre at the suburb of Geiselgasteig near the forest of Grünwald in an idyllic landscape on the Isar, is indisputably Germany's best, with its excellent facilities for both television and feature films.

Artistically, the very lack of an established tradition has worked wonders; allowing men like Rainer Werner Fassbinder and Werner Herzog, co-leaders of the New Wave, to make films that owe little to Germany's cinematographic past. They have taken to extremes the techniques exploited by France's *cinéma vérité*—long-held shots, stark light-and-shadow tones, fragmented dialogue. But the young directors of the Munich school have gone even further, backing away completely from the formal approach to direction. They have an aversion to employing professional actors, prefer-

Visitors to the Deutsches Museum, Munich's museum of science and technology, examine some aeroplane exhibits that include the reconstructed red Fokker DR 1 thought to have been flown by First World War air ace Manfred von Richthofen, fondly nicknamed "the Red Baron". Below, on the ground floor, model ships illustrate the evolution of marine navigation.

ring to use what they call "real people", inexperienced in films, who are encouraged to work out the purpose of the scene for themselves, often without rehearsal. Improvisation is the key, both in acting and direction.

With these techniques, often very demanding on the viewer, Munich's directors have explored themes previously neglected in Germany—the burden of recent history, the impact of terrorism, the materialism of the postwar world, the stultifying effects of conventional ways of life. There is, as you may guess, little comedy in Germany's New Wave.

Though several of Munich's directors have jointly set up their own finance company, the Filmverlag der Autoren, the Munich school is not a unified one. There is no central point, no leader, little swapping of ideas. In 1976 Ingmar Bergman, the great Swedish director, moved to Munich and there was a brief flurry of rumour that perhaps the city's film-makers might find a spiritual leader. Not a bit of it; Bergman made no effort to seek out Munich's directors. He was as happy chatting with Franz Josef Strauss as with colleagues. It is the same with Munich's own film-makers; perhaps because everybody is so busy with his own project, there is little exchange of ideas. "When I see Fassbinder," says Herzog, "I say something like 'I like what you are wearing'. After that, I don't know what to say."

Herzog, with a drooping moustache and sad brown eyes, is as eccentric in his personal life as in his films. In 1974 he walked 600 miles from Munich to Paris—a dramatic journey undertaken simply to pay tribute to the renowned German film historian, Lotte Eisner, who lay ill in a Paris hospital.

In order to film his weird *Even Dwarfs Started Small* in which a reformatory of criminal dwarfs revolt against their jailers, Herzog had to gather a cast of dwarfs who were amateur actors; as the filming stretched on and on, the whole cast grew increasingly desperate until finally, Herzog promised that if they only managed to finish making the film he would celebrate by leaping into a pile of cacti. That was an offer no one could refuse; the film was finished; Herzog made his promised jump, and then had to spend days pulling cactus spines out of his legs.

Herzog made his name internationally with *Aguirre, Wrath of God*, in which he chronicles Gonzalo Pizarro's 1539 expedition up the Amazon in search of the gold of El Dorado. I have a friend who knows Herzog and when I asked him about Herzog's reputation for eccentricity, he said: "Yes. But there's much more to him than that. He's an extraordinary combination of shyness and arrogance—except that he doesn't see it as arrogance, but as an accurate view of his own worth. Perhaps he's right. Once I was at a private screening of *Aguirre*. In the opening scene thousands of Peruvian extras swarm, ant-like, up a rock face. As we watched he leant over to me and said, absolutely dead-pan, 'This shot is going to make history.' Later, after the film was released, I repeated his story, with its apparently extraordinary claim, to an acquaintance. He nodded sagely. 'You know,' he said, 'half the film industry agrees with Herzog'."

Women shoppers stroll through an exclusive pedestrian mall built near the Residenz in 1978 with a striking design of Italianate lattice-work and marble tiles. Displaying costly and elegant clothing, the shop windows are clear evidence of Munich's status as a centre of fashion.

In 1975 his *Enigma of Kaspar Hauser*, about a man deprived since birth of all human contact who suddenly appeared in Nuremberg in 1830, was awarded the Grand Special Jury Prize at the Cannes Film Festival. Typically for Herzog, the main part was played by a man known only as Bruno S., who was without any acting experience and who had spent most of his life in institutions. In the film this novel piece of casting completes, in agonizing realism, the alienation of the enigmatic Hauser from society.

Fassbinder, who dresses in a leather jacket and jeans, and tends to look somewhat like a Hell's Angel, is one of the world's most prolific film-makers. He started in Munich at the age of 21 in 1967, forming first an iconoclastic fringe theatre group, then his own unit, *Anti-Theater*, which later became his film-making ensemble. Best known for his *Marriage of Maria Braun*, his concerns are with alienated individuals and the uses and abuses of power, especially the power exercised by love—a theme of particular significance to himself as a self-proclaimed homosexual.

One early film, *Katzelmacher*—an abusive Bavarian term for foreigner—combines the theme of destructive love with a setting and storyline close to the conscience of Münchners. A Greek immigrant worker, played by Fassbinder himself, illiterate and inarticulate, arrives in a provincial town near Munich. The women are attracted to him, but the men despise him, and brutally beat him up. In another film, *Fear Eats the Soul*, he examines a similar theme, telling the story of a love affair between a young immigrant worker and a middle-aged woman.

Success, naturally, brings with it the possibility that the best artists will go where they are most appreciated. Most German directors feel some desire to work in the United States, with its greater experience, greater readiness to finance films and its wider market for their distribution. All of them seem to feel oppressed both by Germany's immediate past and by the materialism of the country. Fassbinder has constantly talked about moving to New York. Herzog says, "I am still looking for dignified places for men to live," and carries his search all over the world—to Britain, the United States, the Sudan, Mexico and Greece. But it seems unlikely, if Munich's magnetism is anything to go by, that they will be able to escape permanently from the city that nurtured their revolutionary individualism.

Munich's individuality is also reflected in the variety of its distinct but overlapping communities. The city's growth after the war has mainly been fuelled by outsiders—not just the refugees from other parts of Germany, but also foreign workers, mostly from the Mediterranean countries, and political refugees, mainly from Eastern Europe. In 1980 there were some 210,000 foreigners resident in Munich, and a mere 30 per cent of the city's inhabitants had actually been born there.

The city's need for labour has mirrored the nation's need during its post-war "economic miracle". In response to the federal government's policy of

Pleasure craft ply the waters of the Chiemsee in the foothills of the Alps—one of many natural attractions in Munich's beautiful surrounding countryside.

allowing immigrants to take up the slack in the labour market, *Gastarbeiter* (guest workers), as they are known, flooded into Munich. Of West Germany's 2.2 million *Gastarbeiter*—mainly Yugoslavs, Turks, Italians and Greeks—130,000 reside in Munich, forming a new class of labourers who live semi-permanently as expatriates.

This social experiment on a grand scale has, in many ways, been startlingly successful. It has benefited the German economy, enriched the countries of origin of the *Gastarbeiter* with wages remitted back home, and allows Germany to "export unemployment" by sending workers home at the end of their contracts if the economy takes a down-turn. But on a human level there are problems. *Gastarbeiter* are second-class citizens, and prejudice against them is not uncommon (hence Fassbinder's concern in *Katzelmacher*). The very term *Gastarbeiter*, once a studiedly objective word, now sounds pejorative to German ears, and the more neutral *Ausländische Arbeitnehmer* (foreign employees) is officially preferred.

In addition to the *Gastarbeiter*, there are many former refugees from Eastern Europe—Russians, Hungarians, Romanians, Bulgarians, Poles and Czechs, each forming communities between 500 and 3,000 strong. The university has its own Hungarian section, one of about six of its kind outside Hungary. There has been a Ukrainian Free University in the city since 1921. At one time in the 1970s, Munich's police listed more than 90 national *émigré* organizations—all from countries behind the Iron Curtain, including 44 groups from the U.S.S.R.

Many *émigré* organizations maintain their own underground networks, smuggling people and goods in and out of their home countries. The security problems for the Munich police are enormous. It is impossible, for example, to establish motives in many of the murder cases in the *émigré* communities, some of which have been spectacular and have attracted international attention. In 1957, Lev Rebet, a Ukrainian nationalist, was killed in the hallway to his office on the Karlsplatz by a poison gas-pellet that exploded in his face at point-blank range. Two years later, in October 1959, the best known of the Ukrainian partisans, Stepan Bandera, died mysteriously in Munich, apparently in the same way. A few years afterwards, another Ukrainian, Bogdan Stashinsky, turned himself in to the police claiming he was the murderer of the two victims on assignment as a trained K.G.B. agent. Stashinsky was tried and sentenced to life imprisonment. His gas-pellet pistol was a tabloid sensation for several days.

Given Munich's unofficial status as capital of Europe's *émigrés*, it was natural that, when in 1951 America's C.I.A. decided to set up two radio stations as part of its propaganda operations in Europe, it chose Munich as a base. The two stations, Radio Free Europe and Radio Liberty, were established to broadcast not only *to*, but also *about*, the Communist world beyond the Iron Curtain, and they have been doing so ever since. Radio Liberty broadcasts to the U.S.S.R. for more than 400 hours per week in the

At a high society wedding reception on a private estate at Aschau, south-east of Munich, a group of horn players provides hunting tunes and calls to accompany the festivities. Such groups are in frequent demand for weddings, especially those at the homes of Bavaria's landed aristocracy.

15 main languages of the Soviet Union, from a 24-hour Russian service to half an hour in Kazak Turkmen. Radio Free Europe concentrates on the other countries of Eastern Europe, with as much as 20 hours daily in its three main languages, Polish, Hungarian and Czech. The two stations, which merged their organizations in 1976, now have a staff of 1,700. They are no longer controlled by the C.I.A., but by a presidentially appointed Board for International Broadcasting in Washington, D.C.

Because of its patchwork of foreign communities, Munich is sometimes referred to as a melting-pot. But it is a false analogy. The various groups keep very much to themselves. This should not be surprising, for Munich's individuality is in part the product of the individuality of all its elements, by which I mean not simply the foreigners, but also a fair proportion of Münchners, many of whom form their own introverted groups.

At the top, inevitably, there is a small band of élitists who figure on the guest list of dinner parties given by members of the aristocracy and wealthy industrialists. The aristocrats, some 2,600 of them, attend each other's parties, the women still occasionally donning their tiaras for a wedding reception. Munich's gilded youth rock away the nights at discos like Namenlos and Sugar Shack; while journalists drink in Harry's New York bar; literati meet at the Authors' Bookshop; businessmen have lunch at Boettner's; and students gather in Haidhausen, the latter-day Schwabing, carefree, before having to take life seriously in Frankfurt or the Rhineland.

One group that does, unusually for Munich, involve people of various backgrounds is Munich's self-elected jet set, whose lavish functions fill Germany's tabloids almost weekly. At these parties, industrialists and aristocrats, *arrivistes* and writers rub shoulders. Here you may see the wealthy and established members of Munich society chatting with fashionable young starlets—observed, perhaps, by a gossip columnist from one of the newspapers. And here you can also meet pseudo-aristocrats, society climbers who have done business with one of Munich's most extraordinary characters, "Consul" Hans Weyer. The self-appointed "Consul", who was once financial adviser to the President of Liberia and sports 18 decorations from an assortment of South American countries, has made his living in part by buying titles from the *anciens pauvres* and selling them to the *nouveaux riches.* He has, inevitably, written a best-seller about his colourful life, entitled *Schwarzrotgold Titel Träger* (The Bearer of Black, Red and Golden Titles).

This is the new Munich society, an aristocracy of wealth and position, and, as everywhere, it can easily be derided. But to do so seems a little harsh; wealth, especially new wealth, finds similar expression in all great cities. It would be strange indeed if Munich were an exception.

But the lifestyle of these small introverted circles of foreigners and Germans is by no means typical of the city. Münchners generally are convivial people, steeped as they still are in rural traditions. As I have already ob-

Enjoying a fine summer's afternoon on the beautiful River Isar, groups of 50 to 60 Münchners ride giant log rafts downriver from Wolfratshausen to Munich, 17 miles away. Much blaring of bands, singing and drinking of beer make this a peculiarly Bavarian pastime.

served, the atmosphere of the Bavarian countryside permeates the city—not simply in the physical look of the place with its rushing river and its green spaces, but in the very nature of indigenous Münchners. Their love of beer, their festivals, songs and traditional costumes, all testify to the rural origins of so many of Munich's ways. Many a town house, for example, boasts the wood-panelling and ornamentation that are typical of Bavarian country architecture.

It is this tradition that has welded those Münchners who have been born and bred in the city into a society that is both tightly knit and hospitable to outsiders; where people are linked by a dialect that makes no class distinctions, and by attitudes that still owe much to the countryside as well as to the urban lifestyle of a prosperous postwar city.

This special, and enduring, interplay of town and country, so rare in modern metropolises, is part of the magnetism Munich exerts on the many people who choose to go and live there. The relationship between the two underlies not only attitudes and ways of life, but also many of the occasions on which Münchners take their pleasures together.

At weekends, for instance, the city is not just a gateway to the south, it is a gateway to some of the most beautiful countryside in the world. In winter, in the grey light of dawn, skiers of all ages and backgrounds muffle themselves against the cold to cart their equipment to the railway station or to their cars. In summer, thousands head out of town to climb and walk in the mountains or swim and sail in the lakes. The Chiemsee, 42 miles to the south-east, is little more than an hour away by car, and both the Ammersee and the Starnberger See (Starnberg Lake) a few miles to the south-west, are within easy reach on the city railway.

There is one popular weekend event that is unique to the city. Its individual elements can be offered as a simple, if somewhat unusual, recipe for a happy summer's day:

Take 15 or 20 giant pine logs;
Truss well with several cross-pieces.
Toss resulting raft in River Isar,
Now add as many as 60 Bavarians;
Mix gently;
Lubricate with beer, to taste.
Baste with an oompah band.
Set adrift in Isar current;
Simmer gently in sun for six to seven hours.

This singular pastime, inspired by the ancient practice of floating pine logs downriver to local sawmills, began in the 1960s. Now some dozen rafts, operated by private companies, ply their way from Wolfratshausen, 17 miles upriver, to the centre of Munich. For about 100 marks ($55) you join a group on one of the crude structures, which typically measure 50 feet by 26 feet. Water sloshes up over the logs. You drink beer, eat Würst, listen to the raft's band, and perhaps help guide the cumbersome craft with one of the two long steering oars until you reach the landing in Munich. There, the rafts are dismantled and taken back to the starting-place by truck to begin the journey all over again.

For the truest flavour of Münchners together, however, I would choose to be with them while they are indulging themselves in their most traditional way. Of all the well-attended beer-halls and beer gardens in Munich, I like best to be at the one by the Chinese Tower in the English Garden late on a summer's afternoon. Here, sitting at tables under the trees, the park stretching out all around, one finds a complete cross-section of Münchners at their ease. Amorous students embrace. Old couples unpack bread and *Leberkäs* from their bags. Housewives chatter, leaning on their wheeled baskets. Employees from the nearby building occupied by Radio Free Europe and Radio Liberty gossip about the latest international political developments. Dogs frolic and children ride on the old-fashioned carousel with its wooden swans and horses.

Seated together, by chance, at a beer-garden table, a senator may be chatting to a garbage collector; an eminent professor, carefully fishing a stray blossom from his *Helles*, will pass the time of day with a chimney sweep or a car mechanic. People line up to buy more beer and snacks: pretzels, sausages and mustard, or spirals of thinly cut radish. *Fiaker*—old-fashioned horse-drawn carriages—take visitors on tours around the park.

It is a scene repeated countless times every year, in beer gardens the length and breadth of the city. Each time I experience it, I understand anew the seamlessness of traditional Munich society and the joy the city's inhabitants take in their country-town capital. It is, you must agree, Munich at its most timeless and its most idyllic.

Bibliography

Altmann, Wilhelm, ed., *Letters of Richard Wagner (2 vols.).* J. M. Dent & Sons, Ltd., London, 1927.
Biller, Josef H., and Rasp, Hans-Peter, *München Kunst und Kultur Lexikon.* Süddeutscher Verlag GmbH, Munich, 1979.
Corti, Count, *Ludwig I of Bavaria.* Thornton Butterworth Ltd., London, 1938.
Del Mar, Norman, *Richard Strauss, A Critical Commentary on his Life and Works (3 vols.).* Barrie & Rockliff, London, 1962.
Dombart, Theodor, *Schwabing.* Verlag Hanns Lindner, Munich, 1967.
Dube, Wolf-Dieter, *The Munich Gallery, Alte Pinakothek.* Thames & Hudson Ltd., London, 1970.
Dube, Wolf-Dieter, *The Expressionists.* Thames & Hudson Ltd., London, 1972.
Fest, Joachim C., *Hitler.* Penguin Books Limited, Harmondsworth, Middlesex, 1977.
Gordon, Harold J., Jr., *Hitler and the Beer Hall Putsch.* Princeton University Press, Princeton, New Jersey, 1972.
Habel, Heinrich; Merten, Klaus; Petzet, Michael, and von Quast, Siegfried, *Münchener Fassaden.* Prestel-Verlag, Munich, 1974.
Hamilton, Nigel, *The Brothers Mann.* Secker & Warburg, Ltd., London, 1978.
Hederer, Oswald, ed., *Bauten und Plätze in München.* Verlag Georg D. W. Callwey, Munich, 1979.
Hitler, Adolf, *My Struggle.* The Paternoster Library, London, 1936.
Hoffmann, Peter, *Hitler's Personal Security.* The Macmillan Press, Ltd., London, 1979.
Hohoff, Curt, *München.* Prestel-Verlag, Munich, 1970.
Hollweck, Ludwig, *München.* Paul Zsolnay Verlag GmbH, Vienna, 1971.
Hubensteiner, Benno, *Bayerische Geschichte.* Richard Pflaum Verlag, Munich, 1967.
Keefe, Eugene K., et al., *Area Handbook for the Federal Republic of Germany.* U.S. Government Printing Office, Washington, D.C., 1975.
Liess, Andreas, *Carl Orff.* Calder & Boyars, Ltd., London, 1966.
Mann, Thomas, *Buddenbrooks.* Penguin Books Limited, Harmondsworth, Middlesex, 1977.
Mitchell, Allan, *Revolution in Bavaria 1918-1919.* Princeton University Press, Princeton, New Jersey, 1965.
Mühsam, Erich, *Damen und Menschen.* Volk und Buch Verlag, Leipzig, 1949.
Newman, Ernest, *The Life of Richard Wagner; Vol. III 1859-66.* Cassell & Co., Ltd., London, 1945.
Obermeier, Siegfried, *Münchens goldene Jahre 1871-1914.* C. Bertelsmann Verlag, Munich, 1978.
Polyglott, *Travel Guide: Munich.* Polyglott-Verlag, Munich, 1979/80.
Reiser, Rudolf, *Alte Häuser—Grosse Namen.* Verlag F. Bruckmann KG, Munich, 1978.
Roethal, Hans K., *The Blue Rider.* Praeger Publishers, New York, 1971.
Roh, Franz, *German Art in the Twentieth Century.* Thames & Hudson Ltd., London, 1968.
Scholl, Inge, *Six Against Tyranny.* John Murray (Publishers), Ltd., London, 1955.
Selz, Peter, *German Expressionist Painting.* University of California Press Ltd., Berkeley, Los Angeles and London, 1974.
Sparrow, W. J., *Knight of the White Eagle.* Hutchinson & Co. (Publishers) Ltd., London, 1964.
Streicher, Gebhard, *München.* Süddeutscher Verlag GmbH, Munich, 1977.
Taylor, Robert R., *The World in Stone.* University of California Press Ltd., Berkeley, Los Angeles and London, 1974.
Toller, Ernst, *I was a German.* The Bodley Head, Ltd., London, 1934.
Weiss, Peg, *Kandinsky in Munich.* Princeton University Press, Princeton, New Jersey, 1979.
Wheaton, Eliot B., *Prelude to Calamity.* Victor Gollancz Ltd., London, 1968.
Wilberforce, Edward, *Social Life in Munich.* W. H. Allen & Co., Ltd., London, 1864.
Williams, Robert C., *Culture in Exile.* Cornell University Press Ltd., Ithaca and London, 1972.
Wyndham, Horace, *The Magnificent Montez.* Hutchinson & Co. (Publishers) Ltd., London, 1935.

Acknowledgements and Picture Credits

The editors wish to thank the following for their valuable assistance: Mike Brown, London; Bertha Burkert, Munich; Richard Carlisle, Great Bookham, Surrey; Bea Danville, New York; Dr. Wolf-Dieter Dube, Bayerische Staatsgemäldesammlungen, Munich; Dr. Brent Elliott, London; Fremdenverkehrsamt, Munich; Goethe Institute, London; Frederic V. Grunfeld, Majorca; Wolfgang Ketterer, Munich; Karin Key, London; Dr. Robin Lenman, University of Warwick; Dina Lom and John Stapleton, German Federal Film Board, London; Eva Malley, London; John Man, Oxford; Rodney Milnes, *Spectator*, London; Monacensia und Handschriften Abteilung, Städtische Bibliotheken, Munich; Lorenzo Montesi, Florence; Winona O'Connor, London; Mechthild Offermanns, London; Isabelle Overbeck, Munich; Stephan Overbeck, Munich; Dee Pattee, Munich, David Pryce-Jones, London; Prof. Hans S. Reiss, University of Bristol; Harold Rosenthal, editor, *Opera*, London; Dr. Helga Schmoll gen. Eisenwerth, Stadtmuseum, Munich; Adelheid von der Schulenburg, London; Rainer Sohlbank, Munich; Franz Spelman, Munich; Jasmine Spencer, London; Stadtverwaltung, Munich; Hans Tasiemka Archive, London; Peter Vogel, Munich; Stephan Wagner, Munich; West Hill Reference Library, Wandsworth, London; Giles Wordsworth, Weymouth, Dorset; Dr. Armin Zweite, Städtische Galerie im Lenbachhaus, Munich.

Sources for pictures in this book are shown below. Credits for the pictures from left to right are separated by commas; from top to bottom by dashes.
All photographs are by Stefan Moses except: Pages 6—Ashvin Gatha, Kay Reese & Associates, New York. 8, 9—Map by Hunting Surveys Ltd., London (Silhouettes by Norman Bancroft-Hunt, Caterham Hill, Surrey). 11—Süddeutscher Verlag Bilderdienst, Munich. 12, 13—Ashvin Gatha. 18, 19—Courtesy of Stadtmuseum, Munich. 40, 50, 51—Ashvin Gatha. 54, 55—Courtesy of Stadtmuseum, Munich. Photograph by Joachim Blauel, Munich. 58, 59—Ashvin Gatha. 60—Courtesy of Bayerische Staatsgemäldesammlungen, Munich. Photograph by Joachim Blauel. 62, 63, 75-77—Ashvin Gatha. 78—John Bethel, St. Albans, Herts. 82, 83—Bayerische Verwaltung der Staatlichen Schlösser, Gärten und Seen, Munich. 87—Ashvin Gatha. 89—Collection Frederic V. Grunfeld, Majorca. 94—Madeline Winkler-Betzendahl, Munich. 95—Courtesy Carl Orff, Munich. Photograph by Dr. Gerhard Büchtemann, Hamburg. 98—Frederic V. Grunfeld, Majorca. 110—Bildarchiv Preussischer Kulturbesitz, Staatsbibliothek, West Berlin. 115—Collection Frederic V. Grunfeld. Courtesy Julia Grat, Berlin. 116—Courtesy Städtische Galerie im Lenbachhaus, Munich. © by A.D.A.G.P. Paris 1980. Photograph by Joachim Blauel. 121—Collection Frederic V. Grunfeld. Illustration by Thomas Theodor Heine, © by S.P.A.D.E.M. Paris 1980. 123—Thomas Mann Archive, Zurich, Switzerland. 142—Collection Gunn Brinson, London. 144—Süddeutscher Verlag Bilderdienst. 147—Collection Gunn Brinson. 148, 149—Bildarchiv Preussischer Kulturbesitz, Staatsbibliothek. 152, 153—Süddeutscher Verlag Bilderdienst. 155-157—Bildarchiv Preussischer Kulturbesitz, Staatsbibliothek. 159—Süddeutscher Verlag Bilderdienst. 161—Frederic V. Grunfeld. 176, 179, 182, 189-191—Ashvin Gatha.

Index

Numerals in italics indicate a photograph or drawing of the subject mentioned.

Colour reproductions by D.S. Colour Int. Ltd., London and Scan Studios, Dublin.
Filmsetting by C. E. Dawkins (Typesetters) Ltd., London, SE1 1UN.
Printed and bound in Italy by Arnoldo Mondadori, Verona.

I